More Than

A Picture

More Than A Picture

A Picture

Melksham's Roll of Honour

1914–1920

Martyn Gibson

First published in the United Kingdom in 2009
by Grean Publishing

ISBN 978-0-9564083-0-3

Produced by
The Choir Press, Gloucester

"O brother dear, my heart is sore,

As time rolls on, I'll miss you more;

On earth you toiled, and did your best,

We miss you most, who loved you best.

As I think of your picture that hangs on the wall,

Your smile and your welcome I'll often recall;

I miss you and mourn you, in silence unseen,

And dwell on the memories of days that have been."

~❧~

"Farewell dear one; we must leave you.

On Salonika's battlefield;

But as long as life and memory lasts

We will remember you.

We often sit and think of you.

Your name we often recall;

But there's nothing left to answer

But your photo on the wall."

The above poems were published in the Wiltshire Times Newspaper (Reproduced by kind permission) the first one was penned by Petty Officer P.G. Fry in memory of his brother William Victor Fry. The other by the parents of Sergeant Beaven of Union Street, Melksham.

FOREWORD

The Great War touched the lives of countless families of many nations across the world, in this book Martyn Gibson brings the horror of war much closer to home. Starting with the names on Canon Square war memorial and names from other records Martyn has researched the family background and other available public accounts of those who died in action.

Many families and descendants in the Melksham area will gain from the information published here, we are grateful to Martyn for his work. With our armed forces involved in continuing conflicts, this book reminds us all of the sacrifice made by a previous generation and the respect we owe to the present generation in preserving our way of life and values that so many died defending.

Richard Wiltshire
Mayor of Melksham

11th September 2009

ACKNOWLEDGEMENTS

As this book has taken shape over the last couple of years more and more people are owed a debt of gratitude. In response to my request published in the local Melksham News many people came forward to provide me with photographs and personal information on various individuals who served during the Great War. The Melksham and District Historical Society especially Mr J Holness for his permission to use his own research on the war memorial for my own records and Mrs Cathy Berry who kindly supplied pictures of Melksham from the start of the war in 1914 and the victory celebrations in Melksham Market Place in 1918.

The Wiltshire Times editor, Mr Gary Lawrence, for giving me permission to use extracts and photographs from the Wiltshire Times from the period 1914 to 1919.

I would also like to single out The Rifles (Berkshire and Wiltshire) Museum in Salisbury, especially the curator Michael Cornwall for giving me permission to use extracts from the Battalion War Diaries which are available on their web site at www.thewardrobe.org.uk.

In a broader sense many people have also helped to formulate this book from around the country. The advent of the Internet has opened up a whole new world of information and none more so than the Great War Forum on the web site 'The Long Long Trail'. My many requests for information on various individuals or photograph requests of gravestones around the country have been met with unstinting kindness by the members of the forum. Indeed one member, Mr Harry Fecitt, whilst on holiday in Kenya went to the Commonwealth War Graves Commission Taveta military cemetery and took a picture of the headstone of a Melksham soldier who died there during the fighting in Africa. My thanks on these pages to you all don't seem nearly enough.

The following is a list of people, organisations and businesses who very kindly donated money to help towards the printing of this book. Without their very kind donations this book would not have got beyond the research stage. I cannot thank you all enough.

Mr and Mrs G Mattock

Mrs A Gray

Mr and Mrs T Davies

Mr and Mrs S Wood

Mr and Mrs T Strickland

Mr D Male

Mrs K Greenwood

The Rotary Club of Melksham

The Refa Tandoori

INTRODUCTION

In the summer of 1914 few people in Melksham could have envisaged the dramatic events that were about to unfold around them. On the 28th June Archduke Franz Ferdinand was assassinated along side his wife whilst on a visit to Sarajevo in the Balkans. Austria-Hungary declared war on Serbia and Russia began a general mobilisation of its troops after declaring its decision to defend Serbia. The Germans issued an ultimatum to the Russians to stop their movement of all military on the Russian-German border. As no reply was received the Germans declared war on Russia the very next day. Germany then declared war on France on the 3rd Aug and initiated what was known as the 'Schlieffen Plan' this would involve her forces having to move through Belgium as a means to invading France. When Germany ignored Belgian neutrality and started marching her troops through, Great Britain was left with no other option and declared war on the 4th August 1914.

Britain at the time only had a relatively small professional army and it became obvious very quickly that a massive recruitment drive would need to be instigated to raise numbers. Lord Kitchener who became the Minister of War on the 6th Aug 1914 spearheaded the campaign and the now iconic image of him with the pointing finger urging young men to join up was born. There was no shortage of patriotic fervour and this was shown in the large queues of men lining up outside local recruitment halls waiting to enlist. The thought that it could all be over by Christmas added an impetus to join up and get to the front to 'do their bit'. But this was all before the true horror of trench warfare, going over the top and the use of toxic gasses was known.

By the end of the war there would be almost no city, town or village, nor any family that was not touched in some way. Everybody would have known some one who had paid the ultimate sacrifice and lost their life. Men who

Recruits line up in the Market Place 1914
(Pictures courtesy Melksham and District Historical Society)

lost their lives at battles that have now become synonymous with slaughter, Ypres, Passchendaele and perhaps the most infamous of them all, the Somme. But these are not the only locations that men from Melksham served in as this was a truly global conflict. There are the men who joined the Navy and Marines who lost their lives at sea. There are the men who served in the Middle East fighting in what is now Israel and also Iraq, two countries that are today still in the news and enduring conflict. There were the landings on the Gallipoli peninsular in Turkey and there are also those who lost their lives in the African campaigns whilst serving in regiments like the Rhodesian Rifles.

After the end of the war in the 1920's, a new phenomenon appeared all over Britain, the war memorial. They began to appear on village greens, market squares and in churchyards. This was unheard of before because this was the first war that had included not only the military but the civilians also. War was not just waged on the battle fronts or at sea it was also brought into the back gardens of the general populace. Cities were bombed by Zeppelins; coastal towns were subjected to bombardment by German Naval forces, many women workers were killed in ammunition factory accidents. Indeed Melksham had a very productive munitions work in the town. People wanted to remember, they had a desire to remember, never before had there been a loss of life on this scale in a war.

The Melksham War Memorial is situated in Canon Square, a very beautiful and tranquil area close to the Parish Church of St Michael and All Angels, which is located to the left of the Memorial and very close to the centre of Melksham. Today this area takes one back to a different era in Melksham's history with many fine old buildings to be found in the Square. The Memorial was erected to provide a focal point, a visible reminder to those who had died in the service of their country. The vicar of St Michaels Church, Canon Wyld who had lost his only son at the very beginning of the war, had approached others from the town that had also lost loved ones. He asked for donations to try and reach a total of about £200. When this was achieved he himself donated the balance of £150. This gives the memorial the distinction of having been secured by the relatives of those named on the memorial rather than as the town as a whole. The speed with which all of this was accomplished goes some way, I suspect to explaining why there are many others that are not named on the memorial.

There are numerous other reasons for this and many of these I had not even considered until I took up this research. Some families did not accept the loss of a loved one and clung on in hope that they would return from some P.O.W. camp or that they were maybe laid up in some hospital with amnesia. Some did not want to be reminded of the loss of a loved one every time they went past a memorial. Some parents died young and widows remarried and moved away and details were not passed on to the relevant authorities for inclusion on the memorial. Some of those who had died although coming from Melksham had moved away for work reasons. It is a sad sight in the Wiltshire Times of early 1919 where columns of requests for information on missing relations appear. Some hoping beyond hope, that a loved one was still alive somewhere, others just wanting to know what had happened to their loved ones in their final moments.

The Memorial itself is four sided and surmounted by a tall cross made of Doulting stone and its height from the kerbing is between 17ft and 18ft. All the Great War Dead are listed on bronze panels around the base of the cross. The cross was designed and erected by Mr L.A. Turner of London and the base work was carried out by Messrs H Davis and Son of Melksham. The unveiling ceremony was undertaken by Field Marshal Lord Methuen who after a short speech unveiled the memorial plaques to the fallen heroes of Melksham. The proceedings concluded with the National Anthem, the singing being led by a cornet. It is reported in the Wiltshire Times that a large number of beautiful flowers were placed around the memorial. Another interesting little event also took place under the shadow of the memorial when Field Marshal Lord Methuen presented the Distinguished Conduct Medal to Sergeant Vivash.

Since the memorial was erected countless people in Melksham will have walked past it whilst going about their daily lives and maybe have not even noticed it is there. Whilst attending a memorial service it got me wondering about the soldiers whose names appear on the memorial, were they so different to me or to any of the others who were standing around me. So who were they? Where did they come from in Melksham? Where were they serving? And what is their story?

When I initially embarked on this project I copied the names from the memorial in Canon Square with the object of finding out as much as I could about each of them. My two other main sources of information were the Commonwealth War Graves Commission web site and the CD entitled Soldiers Died Great War. The search parameter I used on these was not scientific, I simply typed in 'Melksham' and almost immediately I realised that my task had grown considerably when the search results were returned.

Sometimes researching the individuals has been difficult but in all cases bar one I have at least managed to find a little information about them. Sadly nothing is known about 'Henry Hill' beyond the fact that he was a member of the Methodist Church in town and is listed on their memorial whilst living in Lowbourne. There are over 300 Henry Hills listed on the Commonwealth War Graves Commission web site but I can find nothing that relates any of them to Melksham or links him with the town.

I have identified over 160 casualties with a Melksham connection and I have no doubt that there are many others yet to be found as this is no exact science. The results of my research have shown that the civilians who left Melksham to become soldiers, sailors, airmen or nurses served in every theatre of war. One of the worst days for Melksham casualties was on 31st May 1916 at the Battle of Jutland when four men from the area were killed. Charles Fuller, Charles Bodman

11

and Albert Escott who were onboard HMS Queen Mary and Francis Gore who was serving onboard HMS Invincible.

I have only identified one woman casualty from the area and she was Grace Margaret Marley from The Briars, 11, Sandridge Road. Grace was a Probationer Nurse serving at the 2nd Southern Queen Victoria Auxiliary Hospital at the top of Blackboy Hill in Bristol. She was 23 years old when she died. Some of those who left Melksham to fight and sacrificed their lives made it back to Melksham to be buried, but they are few in number, the majority being buried in France & Flanders where they fell. The Commonwealth War Grave headstones of those in the various Melksham Churches are easily recognisable.

In writing this book I hope that I might remind present generations of the enormous sacrifice made by an earlier generation, encourage an interest in local history and perhaps encourage an interest in the thousands of names on similar memorials throughout the local area.

The two poems reproduced at the beginning of this book are only a couple that I have come across that have the same theme running through them. It is not only that they have lost a loved one it is the fact that all they have left is 'a picture on the wall'. There was no body to grieve over, no burial place to spend quiet contemplation and no chance to say goodbye. I hope once you have read through this book that the men and women who left Melksham to serve their country become a little more than just that 'picture on the wall'.

Lest we forget

Melksham Roll of Honour

1914 ~ 1920

Surname	Forename	Date Died
MAGOR	Arthur Curgenven	17/10/1914
HAWKINS	Cornelius	24/10/1914
JONES	Clifford Llewellyn	24/10/1914
JONES	Henry Thomas	24/10/1914
TRIMNELL	Albert	26/10/1914
BAILEY	Clifford Nelson	30/10/1914
GOSS	Alfred John	01/11/1914
MACE	William George	02/11/1914
WYLD	George Richard	24/12/1914
WALLIS	Kenneth L.B.	30/12/1914
EADES	Ivan Stanley	25/01/1915
COLLIER	Albert Edward	30/01/1915
BARNES	Charles	10/03/1915
GOLDSBOROUGH	Ronald Charles	10/03/1915
DIFFELL	William Frederick	29/03/1915
ATLAY	John Keith	15/04/1915
COLLETT	Frank Stephen	13/05/1915
DODIMEAD	Albert Edward	23/05/1915
HANCOCK	Edward George	25/05/1915
CHIVERS	William Joseph	06/06/1915
PEPLER	Arthur Sidney	15/06/1915
ROGERS	Arthur	15/06/1915
FRY	Albert	15/06/1915
SPENCER	William Herbert	15/06/1915
BARTHOLOMEW	Henry George	16/06/1915
WILLIAMS	Charles Frederick	22/06/1915
SNOOK	Reginald Charles	16/07/1915
CLARK	Ernest	20/08/1915
ARTHURS	Frank Stanley	21/08/1915
GAY	Walter Charles Frank	25/09/1915
WORSDELL	D.F.	25/09/1915
FERGUSON	James Shaw	13/11/1915
GREGORY	Frank	18/11/1915
BRITTAIN	Albert Edward	22/11/1915
GREGORY	Edgar Jesse	22/11/1915
SAWYER	Frederick John	22/11/1915
SHEPPARD	Albert	15/02/1916
BETHELL	Henry James	07/03/1916
SEWARD	Harry	11/03/1916

MANNING	Geoffrey Hayward	06/04/1916
CURNICK	George Christopher	09/04/1916
COLES	Reginald Arthur	24/04/1916
FRY	William Victor	27/04/1916
DEVONISH	Frederick Albert	03/05/1916
SCARLETT	Walter	07/05/1916
CARD	D.H.	08/05/1916
CHANDLER	Frederick George	19/05/1916
GREGORY	John	20/05/1916
BUCKLAND	John Henry	27/05/1916
ESCOTT	A	31/05/1916
BODMAN	Herbert	31/05/1916
FULLER	Charles Edward	31/05/1916
GORE	Francis Cephus	31/05/1916
BIGWOOD	Wilfred Ewart	05/06/1916
ANNAL	John Gerald	15/06/1916
WHITNEY	Thomas Geffrey	15/06/1916
WHITE	Albert Ernest	01/07/1916
LOCHHEAD	Andrew	06/07/1916
HISCOX	Arthur George	30/07/1916
KNEE	Stanley George	18/08/1916
ASH	A	30/08/1916
SMITH	Alfred John	03/09/1916
HARROLD	Charles William H.	05/09/1916
BIGWOOD	William Henry	06/09/1916
PHILLIPS	Sidney George	14/09/1916
RICKETTS	Charles Stanley	05/10/1916
DAY	Ernest Alfred	09/10/1916
MARLEY	Grace Margaret	12/10/1916
REYNOLDS	Herbert Nelson	18/10/1916
WOOTTEN	Albert Charles	05/11/1916
GOULD	Reginald Henry	15/11/1916
YOUNG	William Henry	30/11/1916
CAMPBELL	Harold Fletcher	12/02/1917
MISSEN	Frederick	19/02/1917
CROOK	Cecil	23/02/1917
SHADWELL	William Charles	17/03/1917
SPENCER	William Frederick	24/03/1917
VINCENT	Raymond George	29/03/1917
SKUSE	Fred	30/03/1917
MALE	Walter	31/03/1917
MASLEN	Ernest William	01/04/1917
HAWKINS	Alfred	02/04/1917
MISSEN (MM)	Ernest William	09/04/1917
HILLIER	George	11/04/1917
SHEPPARD	George	14/04/1917

ALLEN	Percy Albert G.	19/04/1917
HITCHENS	Albert Edward	23/04/1917
BAGWELL	Charles	24/04/1917
BEAVEN	Henry Sidney	24/04/1917
DEVERALL	Frederick Blake	26/04/1917
SARTAIN	Harry	28/04/1917
GUNSTONE	Frederick	01/05/1917
GAISFORD	Frederick	03/05/1917
LINTHORN	Bertram Charles	04/05/1917
HAWKINS	Herbert John	09/05/1917
KAYNES	Reginald Genvy	16/05/1917
TRIMMING	Andrew	25/05/1917
BURBIDGE	Andrew	02/06/1917
BROWN	Arthur Roland	06/06/1917
GREGORY	James	20/06/1917
MILNER	Alfred Henry	06/07/1917
CROOK	George	08/06/1917
DICKS	William James	09/07/1917
HORNBLOW	Francis William	14/07/1917
PROSSOR	Frank Cecil	14/07/1917
NICHOLSON	William	31/07/1917
ASHBEE	Frederick	07/08/1917
CANDY	Frank Reginald	14/08/1917
DANCEY	Luther William	16/08/1917
TAYLOR	Herbert	16/08/1917
WEBB	Charlie	06/09/1917
OSBORN	William Frank	18/09/1917
BREWER	Harry	20/09/1917
BARTON	Frank Ernest	25/09/1917
PAYNE	Francis Edgar	11/10/1917
ESCOTT	William Lot	13/10/1917
PEARCE	Robert Henry	26/10/1917
CLIFFORD	Arthur Edwin	06/11/1917
SHARPE	Harry	11/11/1917
MALE	Roy Douglas	13/11/1917
HILLIER	Henry	14/11/1917
ALFORD	John Henry	22/11/1917
CLARK	Walter Samuel	25/11/1917
BURBIDGE	Walter Francis V.	30/11/1917
TRUEMAN	William	30/11/1917
AMSBURY	Daniel P.J.	01/12/1917
WAREHAM	Albert	03/12/1917
GAY	William	13/12/1917
HARDY	Adolphus A.C.	24/01/1918
BULL	George	16/02/1918
OGLE	Harry Charles	21/03/1918

AWDRY (DSO)	Charles Selwyn	24/03/1918
COTTLE	Bernard Newman	24/03/1918
WHITE	George	30/03/1918
RICHARDS	Frederick	02/04/1918
COTTLE	Frederick James	05/04/1918
HARDING	George Frederick	10/04/1918
KEEN	Roland John	10/04/1918
MOBEY	Francis Richard	10/04/1918
HALE	Ernest George	12/04/1918
RANDALL	Percy Reginald	14/04/1918
LOVE	Samuel	26/04/1918
MERRETT	Arthur Stanley	27/04/1918
EDWARDS	William George	10/05/1918
LODER	William Victor	10/05/1918
NEWMAN	Ralph	21/05/1918
CAINEY	George	27/05/1918
BODMAN	John Cecil	30/05/1918
HELLINGS	Sidney Hugh	31/05/1918
BREWER	Herbert James	01/06/1918
SYDEE	Frederick Percy	20/06/1918
HAINES	William Henry	03/07/1918
HAYWARD	Edwin George	07/07/1918
GODWIN	Arthur William	17/07/1918
TAYLOR	Edward Forster	18/07/1918
FARMER	William George	20/07/1918
TYLER	Charles Havelock	10/08/1918
FLOWER	Sydney	21/08/1918
LITTLE	Clifford Victor	23/08/1918
SMITH	Harry	23/08/1918
PARFITT	Herbert	24/08/1918
RICKETTS	Albert	27/08/1918
SHADWELL	Frederick William	16/09/1918
BURBIDGE	Thomas Harold	19/09/1918
YOUNG	Frederick	22/09/1918
PARK	Sydney Alfred	28/09/1918
WEBB	Harry	30/09/1918
ALFORD	Victor Wallace	01/10/1918
ASH	Reginald	02/10/1918
WALKER	William Henry	03/10/1918
GRANT	Hedley Alexander	04/10/1918
GREGORY	Ernest Albert	09/10/1918
MATTOCK	William A.	11/10/1918
PARSONS	Arthur Leslie	12/10/1918
SALTER	Walter	17/10/1918
BAKER	Victor	18/10/1918
GUNSTONE	William Henry	20/10/1918

ELLIS	Reginald Bertram	01/11/1918
COOK	William John	02/11/1918
SPARKS	Bertie	02/11/1918
HATHERALL	William	09/11/1918
WHITING	Percy Louis	24/11/1918
CLEVERLY	William John	26/11/1918
SMITH	Sydney Bicheno	01/12/1918
MERCHANT	Herbert John	05/12/1918
ALEXANDER	Alfred Henry	08/12/1018
FRANKCOM	Ronald Claude	14/01/1919
ROGERS	E.	10/03/1919
ELLERY	Robert James	05/07/1919
NORRIS	Frederick Guy	06/07/1919
PARK	C.	09/09/1919
OWEN	J.A.	06/11/1919
MERRETT	W.F.	25/03/1920
HILL	H	Date Unknown

R/1293 Able Seaman John Henry ALFORD Royal Naval Volunteer Reserve. Nelson Battalion Royal Naval Division

John Alford was born on 9th July 1886. He was on the Army reserve from 11th December 1915 and entered active service on 25th April 1917. He was drafted to the Western Front on the 9th July 1917 joining Nelson Battalion of the Royal Naval Division. On 22nd November 1917 during the 3rd Ypres more infamously known as the Battle of Passchendaele, Able Seaman John Henry Alford died in

12th General Hospital, Rouen, of wounds received in action on 29th October 1917. He is buried in St Sever Cemetery Extension Rouen. Memorial P.III.P10B. Commemorated on the Avon Employees Memorial Nelson Battalion had moved into the line for 24 hours and about twenty men were killed in Action or Died of Wounds during this short period. The RND were operating in an area of swamp on the left of the ridge running towards Passchendaele.

"Pte J Alford was one of the men formerly employed at the Avon Rubber Works, Melksham, whose lives have been given in the service of their country in France. He was attached to the Royal Naval Division and was seriously wounded by a gun shot on October 29th. He was well known in Melksham where he was a prominent figure on the football field and was much respected by the many who knew him. He was a son of Mr Thomas Alford, resided at West Hill, Whitley and was about 30 years of age. Much sympathy is felt for his family and friends, particularly the widow, who is left with a young child. Mrs Alford (nee Miss Hawkins, of Bowerhill) in addition to her husband has lost three brothers in the war and has three brothers now serving. About 40 of the men previously working for the Avon Rubber Company have sacrificed their lives since the outbreak of hostilities.
Mrs J Alford & Mr and Mrs T Alford & Family wish to return their heartfelt thanks to the many friends who have shown sympathy with them in the sad bereavement they have sustained through the death on active service of Private J Alford."
(Picture and text courtesy Wiltshire Times)

27601 Private Daniel Pearce James AMSBURY, 2nd Battalion Grenadier Guards

Died on the1st December 1917 aged 30. Son of Robert Pearce James Amsbury and Harriet Elizabeth Amsbury, of Pleasant Rd., Staple Hill, Bristol; husband of Hebe Frances Amsbury, of Victoria Cottage, Semington Rd., Melksham, Wiltshire. Buried in Bailleul Road East Cemetery, St Laurent-Blangy, Pas de Calais, France. Plot IV. Row G. Grave 27.

The 2nd Battalion attacked Gauche Wood, near Villers-Guislain, just after 6.30 a.m. on the 1st December, 1917. The wood was defended by machine guns and the Grenadiers had to make a dash uphill over 1200 yards to the edge of the wood. Amazingly, they did not sustain too many casualties until nearly in the wood and then hand to hand bayonet fighting took place. The attack was successful but casualties were 153 killed, wounded or missing.

 2718 Private John Gerald ANNAL, 1st/4th Battalion Somerset Light Infantry

Died on the 15th June 1916, as a Prisoner of War at Mosul. He has no known grave. Commemorated on the Basra Memorial, Iraq. Panel 12. Commemorated on the plaque in the United Reform Church and on his parents headstone in Melksham Cemetery.

 8433 Private Frank Stanley ARTHURS, 2nd Battalion King's Shropshire Light Infantry

Killed in Action 21st August 1915. Son of Alice Naomi Arthur's, of 66, Longridge Rd., Earl's Court, London, and the late Percy Edmund Arthurs. Desplanque Farm Cemetery, La Chapelle-D'Armentieres Ref C14.

 11047 Lance Sergeant John Keith ATLAY 2nd Battalion Duke of Edinburgh's Wiltshire Regiment

Killed in Action on the 15th April 1915 aged 24. Son of Thomas Ware Atlay and Nancie Atlay, of Hilmarton, Calne, Wilts. Buried Rue Du Bois Military Cemetery Fleurbaix II. D. 18.

War Diary Extract Thursday 15th April 1915

A trench mortar fell in 'A' Company's trench about 8pm, killing 2 and wounding 4. This trench was only 100yds from enemy's trench at this point.

 # 8032 Private Charles BARNES, 2nd Battalion Duke of Edinburgh's Wiltshire Regiment

Killed in action on the10th March 1915 aged 24. Born Potterne, enlisted and resident Melksham. Son of Mr. and Mrs. A. Barnes, of 3, Selfe Cottages, Beanacre Rd., Melksham. He has no known grave and is commemorated on Le Touret Memorial, Pas de Calais, France, Panels 33 and 34.

Extract from War Diary Wednesday 10th March 1915

Battalion paraded at 2.30am near NU MONDE crossroads under Capt Gillson & marched to CAMERON LANE (accompanied by machine guns) The Battalion arrived at the first position of assembly (CAMERON LANE) at 5.30am and occupied the trenches there in rear of 2/Gordons. At 7.30am the artillery bombardment commenced and lasted for 1/2 an hour.

All the morning the British wounded streamed past and it was not till about 1pm that the Battalion received the order to advance.

The advance from the end of CAMERON LANE was carried out by companies in lines of section at 25 yards interval. Order of Coys 'D', 'C', 'A' & 'B'. About 2.30pm on arrival at second support trenches in rear of NEUVE CHAPPELLE the Coys reformed fast then 'D', 'C' Coys pushed forward to old British trench. All this time the Battalion was under shell fire but not very heavy.

Up to this time the Battalion had been in Brigade reserve but now they were given the task of clearing the German trenches on the left of the 2/ Yorks attacked on MIN DU PIETRE & thence connecting with the old British line. For this purpose 'D' & 'C' Coys were pushed forward to the captured German trench about the road junction 250x S of THE MOTED GRANGE.

Here a great delay took place and Capt Gillson went forward to see what the matter was. He was wounded in the leg almost at once so Capt Makin assumed command.

As definite orders had been received that the Brigade was only to advance at the command of the Brigade Commander there was a long delay. The reason for this delay was not known.

When at last the order to advance was given 'C' Coy advanced between the British and German trenches in column of platoon supported by 'D' Coy in the same formation. A bombing party worked along the actual trench. At first all went well and about 108 (including an officer) prisoners surrendered. These were marched off under a party of 'D' Coy. In the meantime 'A' & 'B' Coys had arrived & formed up behind the leading companies.

When the leading company reached a wide wet ditch about 50 yards NE of THE MOTED GRANGE a hot rifle fire was opened from the German trench. Still progress was made for another 100 yards of German trench was captured. It was about this time that Capt Hoare & Lt Spencer was killed. No further progress could be made that day as the left company of the 2/ Yorks was still further in rear. About dusk Battalion HQ was established close to that of the 2/Yorks in the German trench about 150x SE of THE MOTED GRANGE.

During the night 'A' Coy were brought up & proceeded to dig in, in front of the wet ditch & connecting the German & British trench. 'D' Coy did the same but in the rear of the ditch. 'C' Coy did the same in rear of the ditch. 1 Coy of 2/Gordons assisted 'A' Coy to dig the trench 'B' Coy remained in reserve at the road junction.

G/21922 Private Frank Ernest BARTON, 1st Battalion Queen's Royal West Surrey Regiment

Killed in action on the 25th September 1917. He was born Melksham, enlisted in Ealing, Middlesex and was resident in Hanwell, Middlesex. He was formerly 23561 in the East Surrey Regiment. He has no known grave and is commemorated on Tyne Cot Memorial, Zonnebeke, West-Vlaanderen, Belgium. Panels 14 to 17 and 162 to 162A.

 ## 8420 Sergeant Henry Sidney BEAVEN, 7th Battalion Duke of Edinburgh's Wiltshire Regiment

Killed in action in Salonika on the 24th April 1917 aged 33. Born in Chippenham he enlisted in Devizes, and was resident in Melksham. Son of Henry and Amelia Beaven, of Union St, Melksham. He has no known grave and is commemorated on the Doiran Memorial, Greece.

"Sergeant Beaven was the eldest son of Mr and Mrs H Beaven of Union Street, Melksham and served for some time in the ranks of the local Volunteer Corps. He later joined the Regular Army and was attached to the Wilts Regiment. At the outbreak of war he was stationed at Gibraltar, and was almost immediately sent to France. He was twice wounded and was for several months treated in a London Hospital. In 1916 he was sent to Salonika with the Wilts. In April 1917 he was posted as missing and a few days ago news was received to the effect that he was killed in action. He has two brothers serving, one in India and one in Egypt."
(Picture and text above courtesy Wiltshire Times)

Extract from the Battalion War Diary detailing the actions of 'A Coy' to which Sgt Beaven was attached.

On the night of 24th/25th April the Battalion attacked O1 and O2 trenches, 12th HANTS attacked O3, 10th DEVONS PETIT COURONNE.
A Coy. Objective 21-27 (reference "Sketch of Enemy Trenches" South of DOIRAN 1/5000). 'A' Coy left B2 trenches at 2105. There was then strong T.M. fire and field gun fire on our front line. The company went down the PATTY RAVINE in sections in file and formed up in line in the ravine on the N.W slope. The enemy put up a very heavy T.M barrage in the ravine during the whole of this time, which caused many casualties. The company crawled up the slope in line and having got to the top advanced to the wire. Gaps had been cut but it was impossible to get into the trenches owing to M.G fire on left of O1 and heavy rifle fire all along the line and enemy's bombers. Knife

rests had been put up on the parapet behind the main wire and partly blocked the gaps. The Bulgars supports were seen coming down the CT. on left of O1 and the front line was very strongly manned. Our advance was held up and the company was forced to lie down in shell holes in front of the wire. The main party never got through the wire. A few got into the enemy trenches but were not seen again. By this time all the officers had become casualties and Sgt TOWNSEND returned to our lines and reported the situation. He received orders from the company to withdraw and got what was left of them back to our lines, bringing what wounded he could with him. Two Lewis guns were put out of action, one was brought back undamaged.

 ### 2815 Private William Henry BIGWOOD, 1st/4th Battalion Duke of Edinburgh's Wiltshire Regiment

Killed in Action on the 06th September 1916 aged 24. Son of James and Mary Bigwood, of 1, Deramore Row, Commercial Road, Devizes Wilts. Buried Baghdad (North Gate) Cemetery Grave Memorial marker XXI.A.41.

 ### 230994 Stoker 1st Class Herbert BODMAN, Royal Navy, HMS Queen Mary.

Herbert served on board HMS Queen Mary. He was killed in Action on the 31st May 1916 at the Battle of Jutland aged 28. Son of Mr and Mrs William Bodman of Church Street, Melksham, Wiltshire. He is commemorated on Plymouth Naval Memorial Panel 15.

The Queen *Mary* was fired upon from a range of 15,800 to 14,500 yards, from two German Ships. She fought for about 5 minutes before she was hit at around 4.26 when a salvo of shells landed on the forward deck. Reports say there was a dazzling flash of red flame and then a huge explosion blew her apart. Two ships attempted to come to her rescue, Tiger and New Zealand. As they arrived the Queen Mary's propellers could be seen slowing revolving in the air. The ship sank beneath the waves and all that was left was a dark pillar of smoke.
The casualties were 57 officers and 1,209 men killed; 2 officers and 5 men wounded. One officer and one man were subsequently rescued by German destroyers.

 ### 5187 Private Harry BREWER, 28th Australian Imperial Force

Son of George Brewer of Semington Road, Melksham, Wiltshire. Killed in Action on 20th September 1917 at Zonebeke Ridge, France aged 27. Attended Council

School in Melksham and was a Storekeeper in a Wholesale Grocery Stores before leaving England for Australia on 18th July 1913. He was the younger brother of Herbert James Brewer. Harry is described as being 5ft 5ins tall; weighing 130lbs he had a fresh complexion, brown hair and eyes. After enlisting he embarked for the UK aboard ship number 'A23' HMAT Suffolk leaving Freemantle on the 10th October 1916 arriving in Plymouth on 2nd December 1916. After a brief stay in the UK he departed from Folkstone on 21st December 1916 aboard the Princess Clematine arriving in France the next day. He was killed in action on the 20th September 1917 and is remembered on the Ypres Menin Gate Memorial

5563 Private Herbert James BREWER 28th Australian Imperial Force

Son of George Brewer of Semington Road, Melksham, Wiltshire. Died of Wounds 1st June 1918 in France. Attended Council School in Melksham and was employed in the Post office in Melksham before leaving for Australia on 5th September 1910. Older brother of Harry Brewer. Buried Querrieu British Cemetery B27.

Herbert is described as being 5ft 6ins tall; weighing 145lbs he had a fresh complexion, brown hair and eyes. After enlisting he embarked for the UK leaving Freemantle on the 22nd September 1916 arriving in Plymouth on 21st November 1916. After a brief stay in the UK he departed from Folkstone on 21st December 1916 aboard the Princess Clematine arriving in France the next day. His conduct records show he overstayed a leave period in France for 5 days. He was charged with being A.W.O.L. and was subsequently fined 26 days pay for his troubles. On the 1st June 1918 during an aerial bombardment Herbert was wounded in the abdomen and leg, he died later that day.

200315 Private Albert Edward BRITTAIN, 1st/4th Battalion Duke of Edinburgh's Wilshire Regiment

Died of wounds received in Mesopotamia on 22nd November 1915. Aged 23. Born Batheaston, Somerset, enlisted and resident Melksham. Son of Albert and Ellen Brittain, of 21, Church Lane, Forest, Melksham. He has no known grave and is Commemorated on the Basra Memorial, Iraq. Panel 30 and 64. Also commemorated on the Avon Employees Memorial and also on Plaque in the United Reform Church.

"Private Brittain was formerly employed at the Avon India Rubber Works and joined the Wilts Regt in the first few weeks of the war. He went to India in the latter

part of 1914 and later volunteered for service at the Persian Gulf. His wounds were received whilst he was serving with the Dorset Regiment which composed part of the force that unsuccessfully strove to relieve the garrison at Kut-el-Amara. For many months his relatives had no further information beyond the fact that he was wounded. Much sympathy is felt with the bereaved parents."
(Pictures and text courtesy Wiltshire Times)

18521 Lance Corporal Henry John BUCKLAND, 8th Battalion Princess Charlotte of Wales's Royal Berkshire Regiment

Killed in action F&F 27th May 1916. Aged 29. Born Whitley, enlisted Windsor. Son of Henry John and Sabina Buckland, of New Broughton Rd., Melksham. Buried in Loos British Cemetery, Pas de Calais, France. Plot XVIII. Row A. Grave 21.

"Lance-Corporal Buckland was the eldest son of Mr and Mrs H.J. Buckland of New Broughton Road, Melksham. He was well known and much respected both in Melksham and Broughton Gifford. In his younger days he was in the employ of Messrs Flooks and Manning where he served his apprenticeship in the drapery business. He was for

several years a member of the local Volunteer Corps (since known as the Territorials), and was a proficient shot. Latterly he had held a position in the establishment of Messrs Soundy and Farmer drapers etc of Windsor, and in June 1915 he responded to the call to arms and joined the army. He served in the 8th Royal Berks Regiment. Like so many others he has given his life in defence of his country and of the principles of honour and righteousness, being killed in action on May 27th. He was 29 years of age. The esteem in which he was held both in civil life and in the army is perhaps best evidenced by the following letters from the chaplain of his regiment and from his employer."

"Dear Mr Buckland,
Knowing, as you probably do, that we are once more in the firing line, you might not be altogether unprepared for bad news of Lance Corporal Buckland of our battalion (No 18521) but seeing that he has so recently been in hospital, I fear that this new will come to you as a great shock, especially as this time things have

24

been much more serious. On Saturday night the enemy attacked our line, and preceded the attack with a severe bombardment. At the time we had a small party out putting up barbed wire under the direction of an officer. Lance Corporal Buckland was one of them and together with the officers made a gallant stand to keep off the enemy, but I regret to say that while they succeeded in repelling the attack and inflicted loss on the enemy they laid down their own lives in doing it. It was a fine bit of work on the part of these men and all who took part in the fight which was very severe, though confined to a small front. We laid their bodies to rest in a small village just behind the firing line and commended their souls to God's keeping. May he rest in peace and may God comfort and help you in your bereavement. The personal effects that were found on his body will be forwarded to you in the usual way. I only want to send you a message of sympathy from myself and the men of the battalion. We do indeed feel for you in this your hour of affliction. Believe me to be, yours sincerely, Arthur Longden, Chaplain."*

124, 125 Peascod Street, Windsor.
"Dear Mrs Buckland, It was with a feeling of deep sorrow and sympathy for you that I heard of the death of your son. He had gained the esteem and appreciation of a great many friends here, and I had looked forward to the time when he would return to take up his old position with us. Everyone here had a very high opinion of your son; he was so thoroughly upright and trustworthy. You have my deepest sympathy in a great loss you have sustained. Yours very truly, C Farmer."
(Text and Picture courtesy of Wiltshire Times)

Extract from Battalion War Diary Saturday 27 May 1916

2:30AM. Just as the Battalion was standing down after the morning "stand to" one of the sentries in the centre of the line noticed something move in our barbed wire in front of the trench. A shot was fired in the direction of the movement when suddenly a German stood up in the wire and put his hands up. He was called to come in which he did heaving a sigh of relief as he fell into our trench. He had no rifle and no equipment except one of the latest gas helmets. He said that he was a Pioneer and that he had deserted because his Officer had struck him. He seemed to be a superior BOSCHE, well fed and clothed. He was sent to Brigade HQ under an escort. At 1st Corps HQ he gave the most copious information, we have never had a record of a deserter telling so much. He said that he was a deserter from the 9th Pioneer Battalion of the 18th Reserve Division, IXth Reserve Corps. He gave the exact positions of many batteries of artillery and of billets used by the Germans. He also said that a general attack is contemplated by the Germans very shortly with the object of capturing the LOOS SALIENT. A joint attack will be made further south. He said that for the main attack on LOOS one Guards Division had been brought from BELGIUM and that gas cylinders have been installed in saps and shafts along front and support trenches.
10:30PM. The enemy after a short but heavy bombardment attempted a raid on our trenches. Unfortunately a wiring party which was out at the time - under 2nd Lt L.A. KLEMANTASKI - was surprised before they had time to get back into our trenches. Supported by the fire and bombs from the men in the trenches this party succeeded in breaking up the attack and inflicting casualties on the enemy. A copy of the official report of the raid is attached.
Our casualties on this night were:-Killed: - 2nd Lt L.A. KLEMANTASKI. 11 Other Ranks. Wounded:- 16 Other Ranks. 5 dead Germans were brought in and two more were seen lying outside of our wire. We cannot estimate the German wounded but excluding those who came under the fire of our bombs and machine guns, those inflicted by the artillery barrage which was very heavy must have been serious.

24192 Private Andrew BURBIDGE 'D' Company 2nd Battalion Duke of Edinburgh's Wiltshire Regiment

Killed in Action on the 2nd June 1917 aged 20. Son of Frederick and Lucy Burbidge, of Ewart Croft, Potterne, Devizes, Wilts. Casualty Type: Commonwealth War Dead Grave/Memorial Reference: J. 9. Cemetery: Ramparts Cemetery, Lille Gate

37235 Rifleman Walter Francis Victor BURBIDGE, 1st/8th (City of London) Battalion (Post Office Rifles) London Regiment. Attached 1st/5th Battalion (London Rifle Brigade), London Regiment

Killed in action on the 30th November 1917 aged 21. Born in Melksham, enlisted London. Son of Frank and Hester Burbidge, of Semington Rd., Melksham. He has no known grave and is commemorated on Cambrai Memorial, Louveral, Nord, France. Panel 11.

8138 Lance Corporal D.H. CARD, 1st Battalion Duke of Edinburgh's Wiltshire Regiment

Killed in Action on the 8th May 1916 age 28. He is buried Ecoivres military cemetery Mon-St Eloi. Grave ref I.J.21. Son of Mr and Mrs EA Card of Redlynch nr Salisbury, Wilts: Husband of Monica Card of 25 Regent St Clifton Bristol. (This is the only DH Card listed on the Commonwealth War Graves Commission Web Site)

Extract from Battalion War Diary

During the night of 7th/8th the enemy lip of the Common Crater was rifle grenaded, by day the Stokes Gun registered on the place where the enemy had been working during the night. Lieut G E Brown was killed by a sniper as he was looking over the parapet. This officer who transferred to the Battn from the ASC in the middle of January 1916 had done very valuable work in the line previously in April when the Battn was engaged on mining fatigues in this sector. He brought up a Lewis rifle in support of the Sherwood Foresters after the explosion of a mine and did most effective work. Later on Easter Monday on the occasion of the Grange Crater he was slightly wounded in the head by a piece of bomb which penetrated his steel helmet. After wrapping a bandage over the wound he continued bombing and did not go down to the dressing station until much later. In spite of his limited experience of trenches he had displayed great coolness and initiative since being in the line.
At 7.57p.m. the enemy sprang a mine between the old and new craters at the top of Birkin CT. The effect was to fill up the valley between the two craters and prevent the enemy from enfilading our posts. A post of two men was buried and their bodies were not recovered. Ptes Drewitt and

Woodward of D Coy. The near lip was consolidated and a sap pushed out to the North to connect with the crater which was blown up on the 3rd. In addition to the two men buried here was one killed and one wounded. At 8.13p.m. we sprang a mine NE of the top of Grange CT between the two existing craters. This had the effect of obliterating both craters and forming a crescent shaped crater about 45 yds across and 80 yds in length. It was at least 60 feet deep. After the explosion a Lewis rifle was rushed up and enfilading fire brought to bear upon a German working party which was fixing loopholes in the northern lip. Good execution must have been done as work ceased and was not resumed. A sap was run in continuation of Grange CT to the lip and a side cut was made to command the right flank. A further sap ending in a Y shaped fork was run out to the Southern extremity and two loophole plates place in position. There was no casualty. The casualties for the day were:-

Killed Lieut E E Brown, L/Cpl Card D H and Pte Deering G. Missing buried by mine debris Pte Drewitt J and Pte Woodward T. Wounded Ptes Chiddey F, Dixon C F and Ball J E . Wounded, at duty Sgt Mitten W and L/Cpl Grieson H C.

13788 Private Ernest CLARK, 2nd Battalion Duke of Edinburgh's Wilshire Regiment

Died of wounds on the 20th August 1915. Born and resident in Melksham enlisted Devizes. Buried in Chocques Military Cemetery, Pas de Calais, France. Plot I. Row D. Grave 68.

Extract from War Diary Friday 20th August 1915 Festubert

All quiet. Nothing of importance to report. 1 man wounded.

79728 Airman 3RD Class William John CLEVERLY, 43 Squadron, Royal Flying Corps/Royal Air Force

Son of Henry John and Mary Cleverly; husband of Frances Eleanor Cleverly, of Market Place, Melksham, Wilts. William John Cleverly and Frances Eleanor Greenhill married 1906 Melksham , Wiltshire. Died on the 26th November 1918 aged 38. Buried at Kortrijk (St Jan) Communal Cemetery.

"On Tuesday the 26th Pte William John Cleverly R.A.F. fell victim to pneumonia, and passed away at a military hospital at Courtrai , France. The end seems to have come rather suddenly, a telegram having been first received by the deceased's friends to say he was seriously ill, followed shortly after by the intimation that the had passed away. Pte Cleverly was 38 years of age, had served about 18 months in the Army, a good deal of his time in France. He was formerly in business at Melksham as a cycle agent and leaves a widow and four children, as well as a mother, for whom much sympathy is felt. The remains were interred with those of many British comrades in France."
(Text courtesy of Wiltshire Times)

PLY/1918(s) Private Arthur Edwin CLIFFORD Royal Marine Light Infantry 1st RM Battalion RN Division

Killed in Action on the 06th November 1917 aged 19. Enlisted aged 18 years old on the 23rd February 1917. Son of Arthur and Emily Jane Clifford, of 7, Self Cottages, Beanacre Rd., Melksham, Wilts. He has no known grave and is remembered on the memorial at Tyne Cot. Panel 1 and 162A.

 ## PLY/10685 Private Frank Stephen COLLETT, Royal Marine Light Infantry. H.M.S. Goliath

Enlisted 27th February 1901 Killed in Action on the 13th May 1915. Commemorated on the Plymouth Naval Memorial Panel 7.

Born in Melksham in 1878 to Frank and Susan Collett. At the outbreak of world war one HMS Goliath joined the 8th battle squadron of the Channel fleet, then went to Loch Ewe to become Guard ship also covered the landings of Marines at Ostend and then went to the East Indies in September 1914. In November 1914 took part in the operation against the Konigsberg in the Rufiji River and in April 1915 went to the Dardanelle's. While there she supplied gunfire support at Cape Helles during the Gallipoli campaign. She was damaged by Turkish Gun fire on the 28th April and 2nd May 1915. On the night of the 13th May she was torpedoed by the Turkish Motor torpedo boat Muavenet and sank quickly with the loss of 570 men.

10945 Private Albert Edward COLLIER, 2ⁿᵈ Battalion Duke of Edinburgh's Wiltshire Regiment

Died at home in the United Kingdom on the 30th January 1915. Born Westbury, enlisted and resident Melksham. Buried in Brompton Cemetery, London. Grave N. 172868. Commemorated on the Old Broughton Road Baptist Church Memorial

135658 Driver Frederick James COTTLE, 108ᵗʰ Battery, 23ʳᵈ Brigade, Royal Field Artillery

Died of wounds on the 5th April 1918 aged 28. Born in Melksham he enlisted in Trowbridge. The eldest son of Frederick and Adelaide Cottle, of Craysmarsh Farm, Seend, Melksham, Wilts. He is buried in Picquigny British Cemetery, Somme, France. Section A. Grave 16.

240 Private George CROOK, 'A' Company 37th Brigade Australian Imperial Force

George Crook lived at Glenavon, New Broughton Road in Melksham, he was the son of a farmer and attended the County Council School. Some time in his early 20's George emigrated to Australia where he lived on Wickham Road, Moorabbin, Victoria. He listed his occupation as a gardener and was aged 24 years old. His father was listed as Joseph Crook at the same address in Melksham. On 8th February 1916 in Melbourne he enlisted in the Australian Imperial Force was given the service number 240 and was assigned to 'A' Company of the 37th Battalion. His medical records show him to have been 5ft 2ins tall, weighed a 129 lbs, his chest measurements was 36 inch, dark complexion, grey eyes, black hair and his religious denomination was given as a Baptist. His initial enlistment seems pretty normal but his service records do show him as having been Absent Without Leave (AWOL) on the 3rd April 1916 and for this offence his was fined 2 Shillings and 6 pence.

On the 3rd June 1916 George set sail from Melbourne aboard the HMAT Persic arriving in Plymouth on the 25th July 1916. After a period of military training in the UK George set sail for France departing from Southampton on the 22nd November 1916. George was reported Killed in Action on the 8th June 1917. He is commemorated on the Ypres (Menin Gate) Memorial Belgium Panel 29.
There are two records held by the Australian Red Cross in which two of George's comrades recall seeing him dead, near to the objective of the attack at Messines Ridge. A letter was written to his parents by the Regimental Chaplain;

"It was in the great battle of Messines, a splendid victory but only won, as all such are at sacrifice of life, and as is often the case the finest fellows are of those that go down. Your son was one of these, one of the fine fellows that make our victories possible. By the very giving of their lives they do it and how timely they go into it. As their chaplain I know how really and sincerely they were prepared for their ordeal, such interest they showed in the religious side as well as the rest. You can be assured he was ready to face death and they knew what to think about if such opportunity came. He died a hero's death in one of the greatest battles there have ever been. God gave him strength for his time of needs, as he gives to all sorrowing relatives for their sorrow"

Pte George Crook was Mr J Crook's fifth son and 25 years of age. Two other sons of Mr Crook are in France and one is in the Navy.

18919 Private George Christopher CURNICK, 5th Battalion Duke of Edinburgh's Wiltshire Regiment

Killed in action in Mesopotamia on the 9th April 1916 aged 19. He was born in Beanacre, Melksham and in enlisted Trowbridge. Son of Mrs. Bertha Agnes Curnick, of The Common, Broughton Gifford, Melksham. He has no known grave and is commemorated on the Basra Memorial, Iraq. Panel 30 and 64.
He is also commemorated on the Avon Employees memorial.

Extract from Battalion War Diary Sunday 9th April 1916

Advanced 4.20a.m. Direction lost on left owing to sniping and small marsh and Turkish starlights coming from disputed direction. Lost our bearings after machine gunfire. Confusion in darkness. Troops dug in about 650yds from enemy. All day and night lines strengthened by men coming in from front. Many wounded crawled in and many were collected. 18077 Pte. J.H. Nelson and 9842 Pte. W.G. Price displayed conspicuous gallantry and devotion to duty in collecting wounded and evacuating them. They have been recommended for the DCM. Capt Robertson collected Battn. together as far as possible.
Casualties.
Killed:- Lt. Col R.C.B Throckmorton, 2/Lt J.E. Binns, Wounded 2/Lt. V.M.W.W. Vreidenbury, 2/Lt. C.C. Webb.
Missing:- Capt. J.W. Greany DSO, Capt L.W. Murphy, 2/Lt. D.E. Cruikshank afterwards reported wounded, 2/Lt. Gilborne, 2/Lt. H.S. Diggers.
Other ranks:- Killed 21 Wounded 161 Missing 37

301709 Rifleman Luther William DANCEY, 1st/5th London Regiment, London Rifle Brigade

Killed in Action on the 16th August 1917 aged 36. Son of Thomas and Lydia Dancey, of Beanacre Melksham, Wiltshire. Educated at Dauntsey Agricultural School. He has no known grave and is commemorated on the Ypres Menin Gate memorial panel 52 and 54.

301846 Rifleman Ernest Alfred DAY, 1st/5th London Regiment, London Rifle Brigade

Killed in action on the 9th October 1916 aged 18. He was born in Banbury, and enlisted in London. At the time of his enlistment he was resident in Melksham. He was the son of Mr. and Mrs. Alfred Day, of 3, Victoria Terrace, Church Walk, Melksham. Buried in Caterpillar Valley Cemetery, Longueval, Somme, France. Plot XVII. Row H. Grave 5. He is also commemorated on the Avon Employees Memorial.

R/20702 Lance Corporal Frederick Blake DEVERALL, 9th Battalion Kings Royal Rifle Corps

Died on the 26th April 1917 aged 29. Born and resident Trowbridge, he enlisted in Melksham. Son of C. Deverall, of Trowbridge; husband of Minnie Deverall, of 11, West St., Trowbridge. Buried in St. Sever Cemetery Extension, Rouen, Seine-Maritime, France. Section P. Plot I. Row C. Grave 6B.

10951 Gunner William James DICKS, Royal Marine Artillery

Gunner William James Dicks of the Royal Marines was Killed in Action on the 9th July 1917. Gunner Dicks who was 29 years of age was the eldest son of Mr and Mrs John Dicks of, Old Broughton Road, Melksham. In the service, as during his younger days in Melksham when in the employ of Messrs Sawtell at the feather factory, he was popular and was liked by all who knew him. He took part in the Battle of Jutland and was also a member of the racing cutters crew winning the Grand Fleet trophy in 1915. He is commemorated on the Old Broughton Road Baptist Church Memorial.

HMS VANGUARD was at Scapa Flow in the North of Scotland at 11.20 pm on the 9th July when a great explosion occurred in the midst of the Grand Fleet. It is thought the explosion was due to spontaneous ignition of her Cordite. From her crew of 823 men, 804 were killed that night. It was said that all searchlights were switched on immediately but not a thing was to be seen. She took part in the action at the battle of Jutland from beginning to the end and did not suffer any damage or casualties.

3/5802 Private Albert Edward DODIMEAD, 1st Battalion Devonshire Regiment

Killed in action on the 23rd May 1915 aged 23. Born and resident in Melksham, he enlisted in Bath. Son of Eli and Martha Dodimead, of West End, Melksham. Buried in Spoilbank Cemetery, Ypres, West-Vlaanderen, Belgium. Plot I. Row C. Grave 5.

Born in 1892. The family lived in The City by the Red Lion Pub. He enlisted into the 1st Battalion Devonshire Regiment at Bath. Albert had 11 brothers and sisters. Samuel, Louisa Kate & Francis all emigrated to Canada between 1901 and 1907. Margaret Lilian went to Canada then Australia and Eli John went to Australia. Herbert, Amy, Frank, Agnes, Dorothy, Frederick Thomas & Florence all remained in the UK. He is commemorated on the Avon Employees Memorial and on the Old Broughton Road Baptist Church Memorial.

Albert Edward Dodimead

PO14322 Private Albert ESCOTT Royal Marine Light Infantry

Killed in Action on the 31st May 1916 whilst serving on board HMS Queen Mary at the Battle of Jutland. He is commemorated on the Portsmouth Naval Memorial.

205143 Private Sydney FLOWER, 1st Battalion Devonshire Regiment

Killed in action on the 21st August 1918. He enlisted in Trowbridge and was resident Melksham. Son of Mrs. F. Flower, of Snarlton Lane, Melksham. He is buried in Queens Cemetery, Bucquoy, Pas de Calais, France. Plot IV. Row E. Grave 3.

M/340069 Private Ronald Claude FRANKCOM, Royal Army Service Corps/Canadian Corps/Attached Siege Park

Died aged 19 on the 14th January 1919. He is buried in Grave X.9.4. Son of William and Myra Rose Frankcom of Cannington Bridgewater, Somerset. Buried in Brussels Town Cemetery. This is the only R Frankcom listed on the CWGC website

5524 Private Albert FRY, 2nd Battalion Wiltshire Regiment

Born Castle Coombe, Enlisted Devizes, Resident Calne Wiltshire. Killed in Action 15th June 1915. Commemorated on Le Touret Memorial Panels 33 and 34

Extract from War Diary Tuesday 15th June 1915 Givenchy Trenches

During the day trench J7 - I5 was shelled and the defenders (2 platoons of each 'C' & 'D' Coys) suffered a few casualties. At 6pm the battalion commenced to attack the line I12, J14 -J13. On quitting their trenches, the leading companies ('C' & 'D') were subjected to a heavy frontal and enfilade fire, the latter from I4 - I9. As the advance progressed it was enfiladed by machine gun fire from both flanks, on the right from the foot of the hill between I12 & I3, on the left from machine guns concealed in the grass somewhere west of J13 'B' coy followed in support of 'C' & 'D' and occupied J9 -I5. 'A' coy in reserve in Scottish trench. 'A' Company had been kept in reserve intact, as it had orders to make a reconnaissance after the position had been captured, the reconnaissance to be on VIOLAINES. The firing line reached a point about 50 yards west of German trench at J14. There was then only one officer not hit in the two leading companies. At 7.5pm half 'A' company went forward to endeavour to push on the attack which had been held up. This half company with half 'D' company then advanced, and were subjected to enfilade fire from the crater, and could not advance beyond the disused Old German trench.
At 9pm the situation was as follows:-
The regiment was occupying the old German trench, with 'C' & 'D' Coys in front of them, and the trench J7 - I5, and were in touch with the Grenadier Guards on left of J7. Groups from 'C' & 'D' companies were returning to old German trench from the front. Orders were received to
attack the German line at 9.15pm in conjunction with the Bedford Regt & Yorkshire Regt. The time was subsequently altered to 10pm. In order to form up for the attack the companies which were holding the old German trench & were being enfiladed from the right were ordered back to Scottish trench with orders to form up in rear of it to clear the field of fire of the company holding J7 - I5. The order to attack was subsequently cancelled as far as the Regiment was concerned, and instructions were received to hand over the trenches to the Bedford Regt and return to WINDY CORNER. During the action of 15th 16th, the Germans used incendiary bullets, and also sniped the wounded in front of their trenches.

L/4877 Officers Steward 2nd Class William Victor FRY, Royal Navy, H.M.S. Russell

Killed in Action on the 27th April 1916 aged 24. Son of George and Susan Fry of King St, Melksham, Wilts. Malta Capuccini Naval Cemetery 310.

"Another name has to be added to the now rather long list of Melksham men whose lives have been offered as a sacrifice in the service of their country, and it might also be truly added in the cause of God and of justice. William Victor Fry was a few years ago a lad living in Melksham, known and respected by many, not only of his young associates, but elder people as well. He formerly attended the Melksham National School and the Parish Church. He was likewise an active member of the Church Lads' Brigade. After leaving school he was for some time in the service of the Hon Mrs Lopes at Sandridge Park. From thence he proceeded to Wilton and was for some two or three years in the employ of the Earl of Pembroke. He subsequently joined the Royal Navy, in which he had a promising career for some few years, and was doing well as second class officers'

steward on H.M.S. Russell, when that ill fated vessel struck a mine and went down. Victor Fry was unfortunately one of the drowned. As he was universally liked, the sad news has been received with deep regret and much sympathy is felt with the family in their bereavement. A pathetic circumstance is that since the new has come of his death a letter has been received from him written on Good Friday, in which he writes in a cheerful style saying he is in the best of health. His father, Mr George Fry, of King Street, is an old naval man; after nine or ten years' service he was invalided out through defective sight. His only other son is Percival George Fry, petty officer on H.M. Submarine E43, while his daughters (sisters of the deceased) are married one to a soldier and the other to a sailor, several other relatives being likewise connected with the Services."

(*Text courtesy Wiltshire Times*)

1508 Gunner James Shaw FERGUSON Royal Marine Artillery. HMS Cyclops II

Born on 13th August 1861 in Greenock Renfrewshire. He enlisted into the Royal Marine Artillery on 13th August 1880 and he served until discharged on 15th August 1901 having served for 21 years. During this time he saw active service and was awarded the following medals; Egypt Medal with clasps "Tel-el-Kebir" "El-Teb-Tamaai" & "Suakin 1884" & Khedives Bronze Star. He was also awarded 4 Good Conduct badges. He was married on the 1st October 1893 to Dinah Day and they lived in Church Street, Melksham. He also enrolled in the Royal Fleet Reserve on 12th July 1902. When war was declared James was one of the first to rejoin the colours and was with the Royal Marine Artillery Battalion at Ostend on 27th August 1914 and on the 23rd December 1914 he embarked on the HMS "Cyclops II" where he served on the Shore Batteries, at Scapa Flow. He died on 13th November 1915 and is buried in Flotta Parish Churchyard Orkney Islands. Cause of death is recorded as an Accident. His medals from the Great War were issued to his widow on the 29th March 1920.

202147 Private Frederick GAISFORD, 3rd Battalion Central Ontario Regiment Canadian Infantry

Killed in Action on the 3rd May 1917 at the age of 32. He was born on the 27th October 1885. Son of George and Fanny Gaisford of 25 Church Road, Forest Melksham. He has no known grave and is commemorated on the Vimy Memorial.

When Frederick enlisted on Feb 5th 1916 his documentation showed that he was aged 30 years old. He was 5ft 5ins tall, blue eyes, fair hair and fresh complexion. He also had a scar on his chin.

> **PTE. F. GAISFORD KILLED.**
>
> Pte. F. Gaisford is reported killed in action, but no word has been received by Mrs. Thompson, of 31 Givens street, where he previously boarded for five years. He left with a battalion last August and reached France in November. Pte. Gaisford was born in England 27 years ago and had been in Canada for five years. He was employed with the George Rathbones Limited, Northcote avenue. His brother, at 19 Cross street, has tried to enlist, but was rejected as unfit. The rest of his relatives reside in England.
>
> *Toronto Star – May 21st, 1917*

200082 Lance Sergeant William GAY, 1st/4th Duke of Edinburgh's Wiltshire Regiment

Died of wounds 13th December 1917 in Egypt. Aged 25. Born, resident and enlisted Melksham. Son of Matilda Sutcliffe, of Ivy Cottage, Shurnhold, Melksham. Buried in Alexandra Hadra War Memorial Cemetery, Egypt. Plot/Row/Section D. Grave 265. Commemorated on the Avon Employees Memorial.

 18968 Sergeant Arthur William GODWIN, 6th Battalion Duke of Edinburgh's Wiltshire Regiment

 Died in United Kingdom 17th July 1918. Born Beanacre, enlisted Trowbridge, resident Melksham. Buried in north end of new part of Melksham Church Cemetery, Melksham, Wiltshire. Commemorated on the United Reform Church Memorial.

 10941 Private Reginald Charles GOLDSBOROUGH, 2nd Battalion Duke of Edinburgh's Wiltshire Regiment

Killed in action on the 10th March 1915. He was born Bristol, enlisted Devizes, resident Melksham. He has no known grave and is commemorated on Le Touret Memorial, Pas de Calais, France. Panel 33 and 34. Also remembered on the United Reform Church Memorial.

Battalion War Diary for 10th March 1915

Battalion paraded at 2.30am near NU MONDE crossroads under Capt Gillson & marched to CAMERON LANE (accompanied by machine guns) The Battalion arrived at the first position of assembly (CAMERON LANE) at 5.30am and occupied the trenches there in rear of 2/Gordons. At 7.30am the artillery bombardment commenced and lasted for 1/2 an hour
All the morning the British wounded streamed past and it was not till about 1pm that the Battalion

received the order to advance.

The advance from the end of CAMERON LANE was carried out by companies in lines of section at 25 yards interval. Order of Coys 'D', 'C', 'A' & 'B'. About 2.30pm on arrival at second support trenches in rear of NEUVE CHAPPELLE the Coys reformed fast then 'D', 'C' Coys pushed forward to old British trench. All this time the Battalion was under shell fire but not very heavy.

Up to this time the Battalion had been in Brigade reserve but now they were given the task of clearing the German trenches on the left of the 2/ Yorks attacked on MIN DU PIETRE & thence connecting with the old British line. For this purpose 'D' & 'C' Coys were pushed forward to the captured German trench about the road junction 250x S of THE MOTED GRANGE.

Here a great delay took place and Capt Gillson went forward to see what the matter was. He was wounded in the leg almost at once so Capt Makin assumed command.

As definite orders had been received that the Brigade was only to advance at the command of the Brigade Commander there was a long delay. The reason for this delay was not known.

When at last the order to advance was given 'C' Coy advanced between the British and German trenches in column of platoon supported by 'D' Coy in the same formation. A bombing party worked along the actual trench. At first all went well and about 108 (including an officer) prisoners surrendered. These were marched off under a party of 'D' Coy. In the meantime 'A' &'B' Coys had arrived & formed up behind the leading companies.

When the leading company reached a wide wet ditch about 50 yards NE of THE MOTED GRANGE a hot rifle fire was opened from the German trench. Still progress was made for another 100 yards of German trench was captured. It was about this time that Capt Hoare & Lt Spencer was killed. No further progress could be made that day as the left company of the 2/ Yorks was still further in rear. About dusk Battalion HQ was established close to that of the 2/Yorks in the German trench about 150x SE of THE MOTED GRANGE.

During the night 'A' Coy were brought up & proceeded to dig in front of the wet ditch & connecting the German & British trench. 'D' Coy did the same but in the rear of the ditch. 'C' Coy did the same in rear of the ditch. 1 Coy of 2/Gordons assisted 'A' Coy to dig the trench 'B' Coy remained in reserve at the road junction.

J/15630 Able Seaman Francis Cephus GORE, Royal Navy. HMS Invincible.

Killed in Action on the 31st May 1916 aged 22. Son of Alfred and Sarah Gore of Watson's Court, Melksham, Wilts. He was serving aboard H.M.S. Invincible at the Battle of Jutland. He is commemorated on the Portsmouth Naval Memorial Ref 13 and also remembered on the United Reform Church Memorial.

HMS Invincible

7046 Private Reginald Henry GOULD, 15th County of London Battalion, Prince of Wales' Own Civil Service Rifles

PTE. REGINALD H. GOULD.

Killed in Action on the 15th November 1916. Born and enlisted Melksham. Formerly 22252, Somerset Light Infantry. Buried in Larch Wood Railway Cutting Cemetery, Ypres, West-Vlaanderen, Belgium. Plot IV. Row G. Grave 14 also remembered on the United Reform Church Memorial.

"The sad news has come to hand this week that he was killed in action in France on November 15th. A letter received on Monday by his friends from Lieut Davenport in command of his company state that Pte Gould had been killed by a shell in the trenches. After a eulogistic reference to his military service the writer expresses his deep sympathy with the family in their bereavement and adds that it might be some little consolation to them that he was killed instantaneously and suffered no pain. In the list in the "Times" however appeared the name of Pte R.H. Gould as wounded. There were two Gould's mentioned and some doubt was at first entertained as to whether the Lieutenant had sent to the wrong family and a letter of inquiry was forwarded to headquarters. An official communication from Major G.F. Bartlett received on Wednesday put the matter beyond doubt..

Pte Gould was 30 years of age. He was the son of Mr W.H. Gould of Church Walk, Melksham. He was previously employed by Messrs Stratton, Sons & Mead where for some time he had been a trusted and much respected clerk. He was well known in the town and had for many years been associated with the Wesleyan Church. He joined the colours in February last, having at that time been passed for home service only. He was attached to the Somerset Light Infantry but was later transferred to the East Surreys and next to the London Service Rifles. He was regarded as fit for general service and sent to France. Deep sympathy is felt in Melksham for the family who are held in much esteem in their bereavement. A younger brother of the deceased has joined the Colours but is as yet only in training."

(Picture and text courtesy Wiltshire Times)

3127 Private Edgar Jesse GREGORY, 2nd/4th Battalion Duke of Edinburgh's Wiltshire Regiment

Killed in action on the 22nd November 1915 aged 25 whilst serving in Mesopotamia. He was born Melksham, enlisted Trowbridge, resident Bromham, Wiltshire. Son of Noah and Jane Gregory, of Sandridge Lane, Bromham, Chippenham. He has no known grave and is commemorated on the Basra Memorial, Iraq. Panel 30 and 64 also remembered on the Avon Employees Memorial.

"Private Jesse Gregory was the son of Mr and Mrs Noah Gregory and was 25 years of age. He volunteered in the early part of the war, and was drafted to India with the Wilts. He was among those who readily responded to the call for volunteers for the Persian Gulf and here he heroically laid down his life."
(Picture and text courtesy Wiltshire Times)

 156192 Private Ernest Albert GREGORY, 25th Battalion Machine Gun Corps

Killed in action on the 9th October 1918 aged 22. He enlisted in Chippenham, and was at the time resident in Melksham. Son of Mr and Mrs A. Gregory, of Blackmore, Lower Forest, Melksham; husband of M. L. M. Doughty (formerly Gregory), of Stormore, Dilton Marsh, Westbury, Wilts. He was prior to his transfer to the Machine Gun Corp 1640 Duke of Edinburgh's Wiltshire Regiment. He has no known grave and is commemorated on Vis En Artois Memorial, Pas de Calais, France Panel 10.

Ernest originally signed up with the Wiltshire Yeomanry before transferring over to the Machine Gun Corp where he served with his brother George Enos Gregory. He attended schools at Sandridge and Chittoe and was employed as a farm worker prior to enlistment.

Sometime during his service he was wounded as he is seen in this photograph, sent to his brother George, wearing the uniform of a wounded soldier.
(Pictures courtesy Mr Derek Dyer)

10970 Private Frank GREGORY, 9th Battalion Royal Warwickshire Regiment

Born in Sandridge Wiltshire. Enlisted Southwark London. Killed in Action 18th November 1915 at Gallipoli. Buried Azmak Cemetery, Suvla, Turkey.

201551 Private William Henry HAINES, 4th Battalion Duke of Edinburgh's Wiltshire Regiment

Died at home on the 3rd July 1918 aged 20. Enlisted Trowbridge, resident Melksham Forest. Son of Henry and Mary Jane Haines, of 40, Forest Rd., Melksham. Born at Trowbridge. Buried in south end of new part of Melksham Church Cemetery, Melksham, Wiltshire. Commemorated on the Avon Employees memorial.

8286 Acting Corporal Ernest George HALE, 1st Battalion, Duke of Edinburgh's Wiltshire Regiment

Killed in action on the 12th April 1918. He was born in Potterne, enlisted Devizes, resident Melksham. He has no known grave and is commemorated on Ploegstreert Memorial, Comines-Warneton, Hainaut, Belgium Panel 8.

Extract from Battalion War Diary Friday 12th April 1918

Trenches around N Eglise. The Battn took up a position around NEUVE EGLISE. Hostile artillery very active all day. After dusk the Battn marched to BAILLEUL to support the troops fighting to the E of that town, but the Battn was dispatched to hold a position a CRUCIFIX CORNER between NEUVE EGLISE and the RAVELS BERG.
Casualties: Officers Lieut R N Evens, USA RAMC missing.
ORs 4 killed, 16 wounded, 282 missing.

204125 Adolphus Arthur Cyril HARDY, 6th Battalion Duke of Edinburgh's Wiltshire Regiment

Born Sixhills, Leicestershire enlisted and resident in Melksham. Killed in Action on the 24th January 1918 aged 22 years. Son of Mr. and Mrs. A. Hardy, of 8, Scotland Rd., Melksham, Wilts. He is buried in the Fifteen Ravine British Cemetery Villers Plouich. Memorial VII. D. 12. Remembered also in Whitley Methodist Church and on the Avon Employees Memorial.

Extract from Battalion Thursday 24th January 1918

3 Other ranks wounded and 4 Other ranks killed. Inter Company relief 'D' Coy relieving 'B' Coy and 'C' Coy relieving 'A' Coy.

24166 Private Charles William Hayward HARROLD, 1st Battalion Duke of Edinburgh's Wiltshire Regiment

PRIVATE C. W. H. HARROLD.

Wounded in action on the 24th Aug 1916 and died on the 5th September 1916 at the 22nd General Hospital aged 27. Born, resident and enlisted Melksham. He was the only son of Charles and Mary Jane Harrold, of Melksham Forest, Melksham. He is buried in Etaples Military Cemetery, Pas de Calais, France. Plot X. Row B. Grave 13.

"Private C.W. Harrold, as stated in our issue for last week was wounded in France (24th Aug 1916) after only a few weeks military service, his injuries proving fatal a short time

afterwards. Thus one more useful and promising life has been cut off, and the sad news was received with deep and general regret in the town and neighbourhood. We reproduce some of the details given last week. Mr Harrold was until the spring of the present year living with his father at the Forest, assisting him in his business as a baker and grocer, and also cultivating a piece of land. He had no wish to join the colours, and believing there was good reason on business grounds for exemption an appeal was made to the local tribunal with the result that a six month exemption was granted. The Military authorities however, appealed to the Country Tribunal against this decision and it was reversed, Mr Harrold having to go at once. He left his business in April and was attached to the Wilts Regiment. On July 1ˢᵗ after less than three months training he was despatched with others to France. About a fortnight ago he was seriously wounded and letters showed his condition to be critical. His father this week proceeded to London en route for France with the object of visiting him. A telegram was however received stating the he had passed away and the father returned home. The turn for the worse must have been very sudden as it was only on Tuesday that a letter partly written by him was received alluding in the hospital. This was written on Sunday. Private Harrold was 27 years of age and was an only son. He was widely known and was much respected by all who knew him. He attended the Primitive Methodist Chapel. General and very sincere sympathy is felt for his parents and the family, also for Miss Dorothy Cannings daughter of Mr James Cannings of Malthouse Farm to whom the deceased was engaged and would soon have been married. Miss Cannings has received a large number of letters of condolence."

The following will be read with interest:-
No 22 General Hospital
Sept 6ᵗʰ 1916.

Dear Mr and Mrs Harrold,
It is the saddest of all news that I have to convey to you about your son Pte Harrold Wilts Regt who was admitted a few days ago to No 22 General Hospital. He died in hospital at midnight Monday night in spite of all the efforts that were made to save his life. I saw him twice on Monday. The first time he was asleep and the second time we had a little conversation and prayed together at the bed. He was very ill then but we all hoped that that he would recover but to our sorrow he passed away that night, deeply lamented by all who knew him. Your son has made the great sacrifice and I know that your hearts are torn and bleeding but I pray the God of all peace to comfort and console you in these hours of sorrow and distress. These are sad days, days of severe trial but we have faith that God is watching over us and guiding us slowly but surely to a great destiny. Be of good cheer your son has but gone before you and though dead he yet liveth. May God bless you, keep you and comfort you and give you strength to say "Thy will be done". Please accept my deepest sympathy. I can imagine what a great loss it must be to you from my short friendship with your son. He was admired by all, he suffered uncomplainingly and died full of the faith of our Lord Jesus Christ.

Everything that was humanly possible was done for him but God took him to Himself and He knows best. With kindest regards and deepest sympathy.
Yours very sincerely
D.J. Jones
Chaplain to the Forces
(Picture and text above reproduced with kind permission of Wiltshire Times)

Extract from War Diary Thurs 24th August 1916 Leipzig Redoubt

The following operation orders were received in the early morning "The Battn with the 3rd Worcester Regt on our right will join and consolidate the line R.31.C.40.65, 58-76,97 .31.D.0.7., 26,35,64 & 65 - 30" Two Coys off the LN Lancs Regt were placed at the disposal of this Battn. These two Coys were used mostly for carrying ammunition etc up to the front line throughout the operation. An intense artillery bombardment was put on the line R.31.C.40.65 - R.31.D.80.25. And the enemy's defences in an area N off this line at 4.10p.m. The 7th & 75th Bde Stokes mortars bombarded the area R.31.C.40.65, 88,67, 66 40 - 55 and also point 76. At 9.10p.m. In this Battn the attack was carried out by A Coy on left, B Coy in the centre and D Coy on the right. C Coy was in support. A B & D Coys assaulted at 4.10p.m. At 4.12p.m. the artillery barrage lifted Northwards and cleared the line R.31.D.65.30, 64, 35, 26, 17, R.31.C.97.76.58. 40.65 at 4.15p.m. Progress on the extreme left was slow but on the right the position was gained and consolidated immediately. Casualties were heavy, amounting to about 320. Six officers were lost, 2nd Lieut Butler being killed. The enemy shelled out trenches heavily for the rest of the day and night. The CO Lieut Col SS Ogilvie was hit by a bomb on the leg. The wound, however, was slight and he carried on.

 ## M/224948 Private William HATHERALL, Attached 'L' Signal Battalion, Royal Army Service Corps

Died on the 9th November 1918. He was born in Melksham and resident at 35 Scotland Road. He was aged 38 years and 9 months old when he enlisted on 8th Dec 1916. He was according to his medical records in good physical shape although he was in some need of dental treatment according to his medical reports, he was about 5ft 6inches tall. He was married to Lilian Edwina May Hatherall on 25th October 1903 in Camberwell, London. They had three children Gladys, Evelyne and Charles all born in Melksham. William passed away after contracting influenza and pneumonia. He is buried in St Sever Cemetery Extension, Rouen, Seine-Maritime, France. Section S. Plot III. Row FF. Grave 16 also commemorated on the United Reform Church Memorial.

 ## 8651 Private Alfred HAWKINS, 2nd Battalion Duke of Edinburgh's Wiltshire Regiment

Died of wounds on the 2nd April 1917. He was born in Whaddon, Wiltshire, enlisted Devizes, resident Melksham. Buried in Warlincourt Halte British Cemetery, Saulty, Pas de Calais, France. Plot VI. Row G. Grave 9.

21st Brigade attacked HENIN with 21st Division on the right. The 2nd Yorkshire Regt, assisted by two companies of the 19th Manchester Regt got in to the village, but met with strong resistance. They established and consolidated three posts, but were unable to clean the village for some time. About 9.0am "B" company 2nd Wiltshire Regt, were ordered up in support and came under orders of Col EDWARDS, commanding 2nd Yorkshire Regt. Towards nightfall the village was cleared of the enemy, and the position consolidated. During the night the 90th Brigade relieved the garrison of the village, and "B" company 2nd Wiltshire Regt, returned to their original position in the reserve line, having suffered only one casualty. Draft of 25 Or taken on strength but remained at Corps reinforcement Camp.

 ### 3/9874 Private Cornelius HAWKINS, 2nd Battalion Duke of Edinburgh's Wiltshire Regiment

Died on 24th October 1914 he has no known grave and is commemorated on the Ypres Menin Gate Memorial Panel 53.

Extract from War Diary Saturday 24th October 1914 Beselare Belgium

About 5.30am (just before daybreak) the enemy attacked in a very superior force but were driven back with heavy loss. They attacked again, and after about 2 hours of almost continuous fighting in which the enemy lost hundreds in killed and wounded, they broke through the lines having previously contrived to come around on our left through trenches that had been vacated with the exception of about 30 NCOs and men mostly from trenches on right the remainder of Battalion were either killed or captured, a large number being captured. Cpl Alderton who had escaped from trench on left of BECELARE road together with Privates Dunn, Holister and Jones being apparently last to leave the trenches, gathered stragglers together and formed a rear guard to Brigade ambulances by opening out in skirmishing order. On arrival at 7th Divisional HQ he was met by Cpl Bull, and in the evening the APM took party numbering 26 back to Brigade HQ where they met Cpl Richens and 50 men which included about 12 Lance Corporals. The majority of these men had been driven from their trenches by artillery fire the previous evening. The Quarter master hearing that Lieut Macnamara was wounded visited him at the field hospital and afterwards about 4pm collected the 50 men above mentioned taking them to Brigade HQ and was informed that no news of Battalion had been received since early morning.
NOTE : special mention should be made of the gallant worth of Capt Comyn, the medical officer and stretcher bearers who for the last three days and nights were continuously handling wounded or burying dead.

 ### 508233 Sapper Herbert John HAWKINS, 505th Field Company Royal Engineers

Died of wounds on the 9th May 1917. He was born Melksham, enlisted Castle Cary, Somerset. Formerly 3223, Somerset Light Infantry. Buried in Erquinghem-Lys Churchyard Extension, Nord, France. Plot II. Row B. Grave 9.

46799 Private Edwin George HAYWARD, 17th Battalion Lancashire Fusiliers

Killed in Action on the 7th July 1918. Born Sandy Lane Wiltshire, enlisted in Devizes initially as 20697 Pte Hayward in the Royal Army Veterinary Corps. Son of E.G. and Elizabeth Hayward of Manor Farm, Castle Coombe, Chippenham Wilts.
Buried in Lindenhoek Chalet Military Cemetery II.A.5

71209 Private Sydney Hugh HELLINGS, 2nd Battalion Devonshire Regiment

Killed in Action on the 31st May 1918. He was born in Barnstable and enlisted in Trowbridge. He was resident in Melksham and is commemorated on the Soissons Memorial. He is also remembered on the United Reform Church Memorial.
(Picture courtesy Mr & Mrs Heard)

Henry HILL

Despite extensive research I have been unable to positively identify this particular soldier. What is known is that in 1911 he is shown as living in Lowbourne in Melksham with his grandfather, uncle and his two sisters. By trade he was a Smith and he was born in Clutton, Somerset in 1893. Commemorated on the Melksham War memorial and the plaque in the United Reform Church Melksham.

Known Unto God

202086 Private George HILLIER, 2nd/4th Battalion Duke of Edinburgh's Wiltshire Regiment

Died in India on the 11th April 1917. He was born Horton, Wiltshire, enlisted and resident Melksham. He has no known grave and is commemorated on Kirkee 1914-1918 Memorial, India. Face 7.

"Pte George Hillier joined the Wiltshire Regiment on the 11th April 1915 and later on went to India, where he arrived with his regiment on March 5th 1916. Information from the War Office was received by his friends as long ago as April Last that he had died of blood poisoning at Ahmednagar, India, but no details were given and the relatives have in the meantime anxiously waited in the hope of learning more particulars, which up to present have not come to hand.
Pte Hillier, who lived at No 9 Union Street, Melksham, and was for some years employed at the Avon India Rubber Works, was well known. He had nearly reached the age limit being over 41 when he left Melksham. Much sympathy is felt with his relatives and friends. We are asked to say that if anyone can supply any details as to the circumstances of his death his sister and brother will be very grateful."
(Picture and text courtesy Wiltshire Times)

1636 Private Arthur George HISCOX, 2nd/4th Battalion Duke of Edinburgh's Wiltshire Regiment

Died in Mesopotamia on the 30th July 1916. Born Trowbridge, enlisted Chippenham, resident Melksham. He has no known grave and is commemorated on the Basra Memorial, Iraq Panels 30 and 64.

22866 Private Albert Edward HITCHINGS, 21st Company Machine Gun Corps

Killed in action on the 23rd April 1917. He was born and resident in Melksham, enlisted Weymouth. Formerly 10896, Duke of Edinburgh's Wiltshire Regiment. He has no known grave and is commemorated on the Arras Memorial, Pas de

Calais, France Bay 10. He is also remembered on the Avon Employees memorial and also on the United Reform Church Memorial.
(*His name appears as 'Hitchens' on the memorial but as 'Hitchings' on the memorials in the Church and the Avon.)

8741 Private Clifford Llewellyn JONES, 2nd Battalion Duke of Edinburgh's Wiltshire Regiment

Killed in action on the 24th October 1914 aged 22. He was born in Corsham, enlisted Trowbridge, resident Melksham. Son of George Jones of 35, Bank St., Melksham. He has no known grave and is commemorated on the Ypres Menin Gate Memorial, Ieper, West-Vlaanderen, Belgium Panel 53.

Extract from Battalion War Diary Saturday 24th October 1914

About 5.30am (just before daybreak) the enemy attacked in a very superior force but were driven back with heavy loss. They attacked again, and after about 2 hours of almost continuous fighting in which the enemy lost hundreds in killed and wounded, they broke through the lines having previously contrived to come around on our left through trenches that had been vacated with the exception of about 30 NCOs and men mostly from trenches on right the remainder of Battalion were either killed or captured, a large number being captured. Cpl Alderton who had escaped from trench on left of BECELARE road together with Privates Dunn Holister and Jones being apparently last to leave the trenches, gathered stragglers together and formed a rear guard to Brigade ambulances by opening out in skirmishing order. On arrival at 7th Divisional HQ he was met by Cpl Bull, and in the evening the APM took party numbering 26 back to Brigade HQ where they met Cpl Richens and 50 men which included about 12 Lance Corporals. The majority of these men had been driven from their trenches by artillery fire the previous evening. The Quarter master hearing that Lieut Macnamara was wounded visited him at the field hospital and afterwards about 4pm collected the 50 men above mentioned taking them to Brigade HQ and was informed that no news of Battalion had been received since early morning.
NOTE : special mention should be made of the gallant worth of Capt Comyn, the medical officer and stretcher bearers who for the last three days and nights were continuously handling wounded or burying dead.

5160 Private Henry Thomas JONES, 2nd Battalion Duke of Edinburgh's Wiltshire Regiment

Killed in action on the 24th October 1914. He was born in Buckland, Berkshire, enlisted Devizes, resident Melksham. He has no known grave and is commemorated on the Ypres Menin Gate Memorial, Ypres, West-Vlaanderen, Belgium Panel 53. He is also remembered on the Avon Employees Memorial.

1736 Private Stanley George KNEE, 1st/4th Battalion Duke of Edinburgh's Wiltshire Regiment. Attached 2nd Dorset Regiment

Died in Mesopotamia on the 18th August 1916. Born, resident and enlisted Melksham. He is buried in Baghdad North Gate War Cemetery. There is also a Brass plaque on the choir stalls in St Michaels church to his memory.

The 4th Territorial Battalion was under canvas on Salisbury Plain, in August 1914 when war broke out. The battalion was mobilised immediately and embarked for India in September under the command of Lieutenant Colonel Lord Radnor. The battalion mobilised as part of the Wessex Territorial Division, its role being to relieve the Regular battalions in India. The title 1/4th Battalion was assumed as distinct from the 2/4th or 3/4th battalions which were raised subsequently. The 1/4th proceeded to Kenilworth Castle, Delhi as guard to the Viceroy and remained there until April 1917.

Stanley George Knee was born on the 20th April 1892 and was only 24 years old when he died as a Prisoner of War on the 18th August 1916. The tragic news about his death did not reach his parents, Mr and Mrs Alfred Knee of Union Street, Melksham until April 1917. Stan was formerly employed by Mr F Venton in the cycle trade and was for some years a member of the parish church choir. The vicar alluded to his death in his sermon on Sunday 22nd April 1917 and his death was notified on page 1 of the Wiltshire Gazette that week on Thursday 26th April 197 under the headline "Died a Prisoner". The paper gave tribute to Stanley, saying of him:-
"Remarkable quiet and modest in his general character, Private Stanley Knee had a big heart and his death is deeply regretted by everyone who knew him".
Whilst Stan was stationed in India he wrote home saying:
"June 15th 1915"
"Dear ma,
Just a line to let you know I am still alive and keeping well. I received your letter yesterday but not the paper, this is the second week I have not had it so I expect they have got lost somewhere. So pleased to hear Dad is getting on alright now I hope the change will do him good. You might tell Uncle Bert when you are writing to them next time that one of the men by the name of Butler who worked under him at the shop is here with us. He is one of our own men only he was in one of the other company's so I only got to know him when we were on our way out here. We are still in the same place as we were last time I wrote to you. I received Gerts letter and PC last week also a letter and photo from Charlie which I think is a very good one and I am sure he looks more use to a horse than on the first photo he sent me. I had a letter from Billy Phillips last week, they are all having a very good time up in the hills by all accounts, he and
Alf wish to be remembered to all at home. Sorry to hear Bert Lane has been wounded I hope it is not very bad and hope he will soon get over it. How are

Uncle George's boys getting on out there? – do you ever get any new of them now I should like to know if you do. I don't think I have any more to say now. Just remember me to all the people and my love to all at home. Hope you are all keeping well.
Your Loving Son
Stan"

Engraving of the 2nd Dorsets' charge at the Battle of Kut

During Stan's time in India Lieutenant T.N. Arkell lead a draft of the Wiltshire's to serve with the 2nd Dorset's in the Persian Gulf. It was with this Regiment that Stan was to serve with, until General Townshend surrendered his army at Kut to the Turkish Army and Stan was taken as a Prisoner of War. In Mesopotamia, at the southern extremities of the Ottoman Empire, 25,000 British and Indian troops were besieged by 80,000 Turks in Kut. The siege began on the 5th December and the defenders held out for 147 days, waiting in vain for reinforcements to reach them from Basra. The relief force itself was under constant attack as it tried to reach Kut; in a battle at Sheib Sa'ad more than 4.000 of the relieving force were killed or wounded. In Mesopotamia the British were fighting a steady and harsh battle against the Turks, seeking to reach the besieged garrison at Kut, almost unnoticed amid the more accessible war news of the Western Front. The relief force, which Kut was so desperately awaiting, was fighting its way northward, encountering continual Turkish resistance, masterminded by the 72 year old German, Field Marshall von der Goltz. At the battle of Wadi on 5th January 1916, more than 200 British and Indian troops were killed and over 1,400 wounded. Casualties were even higher at the battle of Hana eight days later, where 2,600 of the attackers were either killed or wounded. The battle of Hana was being fought in the hope of relieving the men besieged at Kut. In Kut itself, in contrast to the terrible heat of summer, sleet and any icy wind worsened the plight and morale of the troops, and the many wounded for whom no medical treatment was immediately available. Lying in ankle deep pools amidst a sea of mud, the men suffered terribly. In any history of sufferings endured by the British Army, the collective misery of that night 21st January 1916 is probably without parallel since the Crimea.

On 7th March 1916 the British attempted once more to break through to the besieged soldiers in Kut. The relief force had steadily worked its way forward to a point where it could see the Minarets in the besieged city. However the attack that took place at Dujaila a mere two miles from Kut, failed; 3,500 of the attackers were killed or wounded and the General commanding the relief force, General Aylmer, was sacked. The relief force fell back and the siege of Kut continued relentlessly.

On the 29th April 1916 the British and Indian forces surrenderd. This victory for the Turks was as great as the one three months previous when the allies evacuated the Gallipoli peninsula. Upon surrender Townshends army was lead into captivity, a total of 9,000 troops. Of these 2,500 of the badly wounded were allowed their freedom in return for a similar number of Turkish prisoners.

On 30th April the march into captivity began towards Anatolia. The prisoners were very badly treated during the forced march and were subject to beatings for falling down or falling behind, many had had their boots stolen and were forced to march barefoot. Food and fresh water were not supplied to the prisoners and many died on the march. On their arrival in Baghdad on the 18th May a shocked American consul, Mr Brissell paid money to the Turks to have the worst 500 soldiers sent to a hospital in Basra. Of the 2,500 British soldiers captured at Kut over 1,750 died whilst on the march or due to the appalling conditions they endured at the prisoner of war camps.

Private Stanley George Knee was one those men who endured these atrocious conditions for the final months of his short life. He finally died from enteritis. Stan's body now rests in the Baghdad (North Gate) War Cemetery.

5774 Private Bertram Charles LINTHORN, 3rd Battalion Somerset Light Infantry

Killed on the 4th May 1917. He has no known grave and is commemorated on Savona memorial in Italy.

The **SS *Transylvania*** was a passenger liner of the Cunard subsidiary Anchor Line. She was torpedoed and sunk on May 4th 1917 by the German U-boat U-63 while carrying Allied troops to Egypt and sank with a loss of 412 lives. She was completed in 1914 just prior to the outbreak of World War 1 and she was taken over for service as a troopship upon completion. She was designated by the Navy to carry 200 officers and 2,860 men, besides crew, when she was commissioned in May 1915

She was carrying nearly this number when she left Marseilles for Alexandria on May 3rd, 1917, with an escort of two Japanese destroyers, the Matsu and the Sakaki. At 10 a.m. on the 4th the Transylvania was struck in the port engine room by a torpedo from a submarine. At the time the ship was on a zig zag course at a speed of 14 knots, being two and a half miles S. of Cape Vado, Gulf of Genoa. She at once headed for the land two miles distant, while the Matsu came alongside to take off the troops, the Sakaki meanwhile steaming around to keep the submarine submerged. Twenty minutes later a torpedo was seen coming straight for the destroyer alongside, which saved herself by going astern at full speed.

The torpedo then struck the Transylvania and she sank very quickly, less than an hour having elapsed since she was first hit. Lt. Brennell, one other officer and ten men of the crew, 29 military officers and 373 other ranks were killed.Many bodies of victims were recovered at Savona, and buried two days later, in a special plot in the town cemetery. Others are buried elsewhere in Italy, France, Monaco and Spain. Savona Town Cemetery contains 85 Commonwealth burials from the First World War, all but two of them casualties from the *Transylvania*. Within the cemetery is the Savona Memorial which commemorates a further 275 casualties who died when the *Transylvania* sank, but whose graves are unknown.

2857 *Private Andrew LOCHHEAD, 1st/4th Battalion, Duke of Edinburgh's Wiltshire Regiment. Attached to Oxford and Bucks Light Infantry*

Died in Mesopotamia 6th July 1916. Buried Amara War Cemetery. Born Glasgow, enlisted West Down, Devon, resident Melksham. Son of Andrew Lochhead of Boxwood Cottage, Forest, Melksham, Wiltshire. Also remembered on the United Reform Church Memorial.

PRIVATE ANDREW LOCHHEAD

"Another victim of the war, one, who although not killed with a German or Turkish bullet, has sacrificed his young and promising life in the service of his country, is Pte Andrew Lochhead of the 2/4th Wilts Regiment, who was serving in Mesopotamia. Pte Lochhead, who was 25 years of age, was the youngest son of Mr and Mrs Andrew Lochhead of Boxwood Cottage, Forest, Melksham. By trade he was a printer and served his apprenticeship under the late Mr A.W. Jolliffe at Melksham, afterwards working for Mr Woodward of Devizes and subsequently being in situations at Cheltenham and at Guernsey. In his earlier days he was a member of the Melksham Shooting Club and became a crack shot, winning a number of prizes in competitions. Following in the steps of his father, he remained true to temperance principles, and while at Cheltenham joined a lodge of Good Templars. Wherever he went he won and retained the esteem and respect of all he came into contact with. After the war had broken out he returned to Melksham and joined the Wiltshire Regiment and went with others to India some 18 months since. He subsequently volunteered for active service with the Mesopotomia expedition. He was attached to the 1st Oxford and Bucks Light Infantry and did his full share until he became a victim of the fell disease which has proved fatal in many cases. About three weeks ago his parents received official notification from

the war office that he was in hospital under treatment for enteric fever. On Tuesday news was received that he died in hospital at Basra on July 6th. Mr and Mrs Lochhead and family will receive the deep and sincere sympathy of all who know them in their sad bereavement, the second they have experienced under similar circumstances, their eldest son, John, having died of enteric while serving in the Boer War. Their only other son is Cpl George Lochhead of the Royal Engineers, now a motor cycle despatch rider in France. We join with their Melksham and other friends in the hope that he will return safely from his responsible and perilous duties."
(Picture and text courtesy Wiltshire Times)

 ## 2nd Lt William Victor LODER, 1st/4th Battalion Duke of Edinburgh's Wiltshire Regiment

Killed in action on the 10th May 1918 aged 28. Son of James and Bessie Loder of 47 Roundpond, Melksham, Wilts. He is buried in the Ramleh War Cemetery, Israel. He is also remembered on the United Reform Church Memorial.

Extract from Battalion war Diary Friday 10th May 1918

1320 to 1400. The enemy put heavy barrage on to the forward slope of HILL 1191 and the WADI LEHHAM, including our bivouac area, inflicting a number of casualties by timed HE.
Our casualties were 1 Officer 2/Lt W V Loder Killed, 2 Officers Capt J G Lockhart and Lt B K B Hall wounded.
OR 6 killed and 9 wounded.
Three OR wounded but remained on duty.

 ## 20441 Private Roy Douglas MALE, 1st/4th Battalion Duke of Edinburgh's Wiltshire Regiment

Killed in action in Egypt on the 13th November 1917 aged 25. Born Limpley Stoke, enlisted and resident Melksham. Son of Ronald and Alice Male, of Shurnhold, Melksham. He has no known grave and is commemorated on the Jerusalem Memorial, Israel Panel 44. Also remembered on the Avon Employees memorial.

 ## 202009 Private Walter MALE, Wiltshire Regiment, Attached to 1st/4th Battalion Hampshire Regiment

Killed on 31st March 1917 he is buried in the Baghdad North Gate War Cemetery ref X.H.1. Also remembered on the Avon Employees Memorial.

"Pte Walter Male who death occurred in Mesopotamia was only 21 years of age and single. He was a son of Mr Ronald Male of Shurnold and prior to the war was employed at the Avon India Rubber Works. Like thousands of others on the outbreak of hostilities he showed his patriotism by joining the Army, entering the Wiltshire regiment at Trowbridge in September 1914. Subsequently he proceeded to India and afterwards volunteered for service in the Persian Gulf. Recently he had been attached to the Hampshire Regiment. A letter received by his parents on Wednesday from the Commanding Officer states that he was killed by the accidental explosion of a shell in Mesopotamia on March 31st. Pte Walter Male showed himself a true scion of a good military and naval stock. His father, although never in the regular service, was for a number of years in the old Volunteer Force, and both his grandfathers were in the service for many years on his fathers side in the Royal Navy and on his mother's in the Royal Marine Artillery. He leaves three brothers in the Service, on in the Royal marine Artillery, who has done duty at Delhi and Malta, one in the Royal Field Auxiliary Forces, and one a stoker in the Royal Navy."
(Text courtesy of Wiltshire Times)

 ### 200816 Lance Corporal Geoffrey Hayward MANNING, 2nd/4th Battalion Duke of Edinburgh's Wiltshire Regiment

Killed in action in Mesopotamia on the 6th April 1916 aged 24. Son of Arthur and Mary Manning, High St, Melksham. He has no known grave and is commemorated on the Basra Memorial, Iraq Panels 30 and 64.

 ### 26200 Ernest William MASLEN, 5th Battalion Duke of Edinburgh's Wiltshire Regiment

Died of wounds in Mesopotamia on the 1st April 1917 aged 22. Born in Melksham, enlisted Trowbridge, resident Chippenham. Son of Mr. and Mrs. C. Maslen, of Coburg Square, Spa Rd. Melksham; husband of Mrs. Rose Sparrow (formerly Maslen), of 43, Factory Lane, Chippenham. He has no known grave and is commemorated on the Basra Memorial, Iraq Panels 30 and 64.

"Private Ernest William Maslen was the youngest son of Mr Charles Maslen of Coburg Square, and was until last year the local manager for Eastman's Ltd. He was called up for service in June 1916 and joined the Wiltshire Regiment and in November was sent out to the Persian Gulf. So far as could be learned from the little news received of him he seemed to be getting on all right and his parents and young wife were anxiously looking forward to the time when having done his share towards the victory which is so eagerly anticipated he would return to take up his peaceful duties. These hopes, however, received a rude shock on Wednesday when a letter from the Commanding Officer informed Mrs Maslen

*that her husband died in Mesopotamia on April 1ˢᵗ from wounds received in
action. Pte Maslen was within a day of his 22ⁿᵈ birthday, and his little boy at the
time he joined the forces, was only a few weeks old."*
(Text courtesy of Wiltshire Times)

44197 Private Arthur Stanley MERRETT, 10ᵗʰ Battalion Worcestershire Regiment

Died of wounds on the 27th April 1918. Born Broughton Gifford, enlisted
Devizes, resident Melksham. Buried in Lijssenthoek Military Cemetery,
Poperinge, West-Vlaanderen, Belgium. Plot XXVIII. Row C. Grave 7A.

18345 Driver Alfred Henry MILNER, Royal Field Artillery

Died on the 6ᵗʰ July 1917. He is buried in the Brandhoek Military Cemetery Ref I.
L. 48. Son of William and Elizabeth Georgina Milner of Coburg Lodge, Spa Road
Melksham Wiltshire. Also remembered on the United Reform Church Memorial.

10894 Private Ernest William MISSEN MM, 2ⁿᵈ Battalion Duke of Edinburgh's Wiltshire Regiment

Killed in action on the 9th April 1917 aged 24. Born and
resident Melksham enlisted Devizes. Son of Frank and
Ellen Missen, of "Longleigh", Spa Rd., Melksham.
Awarded the Military Medal (M.M.) for bravery. He has no
known grave and is commemorated on the Arras Memorial,
Pas de Calais, France Bay 7. Also remembered on the
United Reform Church Memorial.

*"Pte Ernest Missen was the son of Mr and Mrs Frank
Missen of Longleigh, Spa Road, Melksham, and in civil life
gained the respect of all with whom he was brought into
contact. When the war broke out he joined the Wiltshire
Regiment and the qualities which gained him the esteem of his
associates in civil life speedily gained for him the respect of officers
and comrades as a true and brave soldier. When he lived at Melksham
he was connected with the Wesleyan Church and was formerly a
scholar in the Sunday school. For several years he was in the employ of*

Messrs T Scott and Son as a Painter and decorator. Since entering the army he had spent over two years in France. He was once wounded but recovered and again entered the fighting line. He had gained the Military medal for distinguished conduct. The news of his death and the regard in which he was held by his comrades was conveyed to his relatives in the following letter from France addressed to his mother dated 16th April:"

Dear Mrs Missen: It is with very great regret that I am writing to inform you of the death of your son no 10894 Pte E Missen. He was killed in action on the 9th April 1917, during an attack on an enemy position. He was killed by a shell and his death must have been absolutely painless. I can hardly express in words the sorrow I feel at his loss as he was a splendid soldier and always did his duty thoroughly and without fear. I wish to offer you my most heartfelt sympathy in your great loss. He will be greatly missed by the officers N.C.O's and men of this company, by all of whom he loved and respected.
Yours very sincerely.
WILLIAM B WOOD 2nd Lieut.
A brother to the deceased solider is serving in Salonika.
(Picture and text courtesy Wiltshire Times)

26659 Private 26659 Frederick MISSEN, 11ᵗʰ Battalion Princess Charlotte of Wales' Royal Berkshire Regiment

Died on the 19th February 1917 aged 39. He was born and enlisted in Melksham. Husband of Ruth Bodman (formerly Missen) of The Common, Broughton Gifford, Melksham. He is buried in Dernancourt Communal Cemetery Extension, Somme, France. Plot V. Row C. Grave 32. Also remembered in the Old Broughton Road Baptist Church

R/38072 Rifleman Harry Charles OGLE, 7ᵗʰ Battalion Kings Royal Rifle Corps

Died on the 21st March 1918 he has no known grave and is commemorated on the Pozieres Memorial Panels 61 to 64. His parents lived in Canon Square and were involved in the church choir.

24520 Private Sydney Alfred PARK, 6th Battalion Duke of Edinburgh's Wiltshire Regiment

Died on the 28th September 1918. Aged 21. Born and resident Melksham enlisted Trowbridge. Son of George and Sarah Park, of 30, Scotland Rd., Melksham. Buried in Cologne Southern Cemetery, Germany. Plot XIII. Row B. Grave 8. Also remembered on the Avon Employees memorial

 ### 203134 Lance Corporal Francis Edgar PAYNE, 6th Battalion Duke of Edinburgh's Wiltshire Regiment

Killed in action on the 11th October 1917 aged 23. He was born in Chilmark, enlisted and resident in Melksham. Son of David James and Sarah Jane Payne, of 64, Church Lane, Forest, Melksham. He has no known grave and is commemorated on the Tyne Cot Memorial, Zonnebeke, West-Vlaanderen, Belgium Panels 119 to 120. He is also remembered on the Avon Employees Memorial.

"Lance Corporal Francis Edgar Payne was killed in France by a shell on Wednesday October 10th. He was 23 years of age and belonged to Melksham being a son of Mr and Mrs D.J. Payne who have charge of the Conservative Club. He was formerly employed at the Avon Rubber Works. For some time before the war he was in the Wiltshire Yeomanry. He was afterward attached to the Wiltshire Regiment and served in France. At the end of his Five years term he came home in July last on leave rejoining and returning to France in the following month. The news of his death which was received with great regret by his many friends in Melksham came to his parents and family through a comrade. A brother of the deceased is now serving with the North Staffordshire regiment in India."
(Picture and text courtesy of Wiltshire Times)

PLY/2031(S) Private Robert Henry PEARCE 1st Royal Marine Battalion, Royal Marine Light Infantry

Killed in action on the 26th October 1917 he has no known grave and is commemorated on the Tyne Cot Memorial Panels 1 and 162A.

"Private R.H. Pearce Royal Marine Light Infantry who was killed in action in France on October 26th last at the age of 32, he was the dearly loved eldest son of Mr and Mrs H Pearce of Broughton Road, Melksham, and the favourite brother of Mrs G.W. Lewis of 4, Orchard Place, Weston Super Mare. He is deeply mourned by his eldest sister (Sis), his mother-in-law, and nephews Leonard and Reggie. A letter was received from an officer says Pte Pearce was a thoroughly good soldier and would be much missed by his officers and comrades. Mrs Lewis to whom the news of his death came as a terrible blow, had not seen her brother for over four years and did not know he was in the Army till in August last a resident of Melksham on a trip to Weston-super-Mare, accidentally met her and told her he was in France. Efforts were made to secure his address and when after some little delay this had been ascertained Mrs Lewis despatched a parcel to him, but two days later he was killed and it consequently never reached him."
(Picture and text courtesy Wiltshire Times)

18224 Private Arthur Sidney PEPLER 2nd Battalion Duke of Edinburgh's Wiltshire Regiment

Killed in action on the 15th June 1915. He was Born and lived in Melksham. He enlisted into the Wiltshire Regiment in Devizes. He has no known grave and is remembered on the Le Touret Memorial at the Pas de Calais on Panels 33 and 34.

War Diary Tues 15th June 1915 – Trenches Givenchy, France.

During the day trench J7 - I5 was shelled and the defenders (2 platoons of each 'C' & 'D' Coys) suffered a few casualties. At 6pm the battalion commenced to attack the line I12, J14 -J13. On quitting their trenches, the leading companies ('C' & 'D') were subjected to a heavy frontal and enfilade fire, the latter from I4 - I9. As the advance progressed it was enfiladed by machine gun fire from both flanks, on the right from the foot of the hill between I12 & I3, on the left from machine guns concealed in the grass somewhere west of J13 'B' coy followed in support of 'C' & 'D' and occupied J9 -15. 'A' coy in reserve in Scottish trench. 'A' Company had been kept in reserve intact, as it had orders to make a reconnaissance after the position had been captured, the reconnaissance to be on VIOLAINES. The firing line reached a point about 50 yards west of German trench at J14. There was then only one officer not hit in the two leading companies.

At 7.5pm half 'A' company went forward to endeavour to push on the attack which had been held up. This half company with half 'D' company then advanced, and were subjected to enfilade fire from the crater, and could not advance beyond the disused Old German trench.

At 9pm the situation was as follows:-

The regiment was occupying the old German trench, with 'C' & 'D' Coys in front of them, and the trench J7 - 15, and were in touch with the Grenadier Guards on left of J7. Groups from 'C' & 'D' companies were returning to old German trench from the front. Orders were received to attack the German line at 9.15pm in conjunction with the Bedford Regt & Yorkshire Regt. The time was subsequently altered to 10pm. In order to form up for the attack the companies which were holding the old German trench & were being enfiladed from the right were ordered back to Scottish trench with orders to form up in rear of it to clear the field of fire of the company holding J7 - 15. The order to attack was subsequently cancelled as far as the Regiment was concerned, and instructions were received to hand over the trenches to the Bedford Regt and return to WINDY CORNER. During the action of 15th 16th, the Germans used incendiary bullets, and also sniped the wounded in front of their trenches.

7657 Rifleman Sidney George PHILLIPS 1st/9th County of London Battalion, Queen Victoria's Rifles, London Regiment

RIFLEMAN GEORGE PHILLIPS.

Killed in action on the 14th September 1916 aged 19 years. Son of Henry and Bertha Phillips, of Avon Cottage, 45, Bath Rd., Melksham. Formerly 5713, 8th Battalion, London Regiment. He was born at Shepton Mallet, Somerset and enlisted and was resident in Melksham. He has no known grave and is commemorated on the Theipval Memorial, Somme, France. Pier and Face 9 C. A Brass plaque in the choir stalls at St Michaels Church also acts as a memorial to him.

"One more young and promising Melksham life has been laid down in the great fight for the cause of humanity and justice. The news was received with much regret, the deceased George Phillips of the Post Office Rifles, being well known and extremely popular. He was a son of Mr Harry Phillips of Bath Road and was only 19 years of age. He enlisted in Melksham and was sent to France at the beginning of July. An official intimation was received this week from the War Office that he was killed in action on the 14th September. The sad news was also conveyed in a sympathetic letter received from a friend in the same corps which spoke in eulogised terms of the deceased and

expressed the regret of his comrades at his death as well as their sympathy with the family in their bereavement. Before joining the Army Phillips was a postman having been in the postal service for some years, commencing a telegraph boy and his genial and obliging nature towards all with whom he came in contact made him a general favourite.

He was also a valued member of the Parish Church choir, in his younger days as a boy treble singer and later as tenor. He possessed an excellent voice which he well knew how to use. He was formerly a scholar the National school and for a time belonged to the Church Lads Brigade.

As a mark of respect to his memory a memorial service was held at the Parish Church on Tuesday afternoon, there being a large attendance of friends and sympathisers. The Vicar (Rev Canon Wyld) conducted the Rev H.J. Webb and the choir being also present. Portions of the burial service were read, special reference to the circumstances being made in the prayers and the hymns selected were "Through all the changing scenes of Life" "Nearer my God to thee" and "Now the labourer's task is over". Miss Wyld presided at the organ and at the close rendered Beethoven's Funeral March. Two brothers of the deceased are serving with the forces. Viz John Phillips with the Royal Engineers in Egypt and William with the Wilts in India."

(Picture and text courtesy Wiltshire Times)

27798 Lance Corporal Frank Cecil PROSSER, 8th Battalion Prince Albert's Somerset Light Infantry

Killed in action on the 14th July 1917. Born and enlisted Trowbirdge, resident Melksham. On initial enlistment he was Formerly 24212, in the Wiltshire Regiment. He has no known grave and is commemorated on the Ypres Menin Gate Memorial, Ypres, West-Vlaanderen, Belgium Panel 21.

23661 Private Herbert Nelson REYNOLDS, 2nd Battalion Duke of Edinburgh's Wiltshire Regiment

Killed in action on the 18th October 1916. Born Trowbridge, enlisted and resident Melksham. He is buried in the Warlencourt British Cemetery, Pas de Calais, France. Plot II. Row D. Grave 14. He is also remembered on the Avon Employees memorial and the Old Broughton Road Baptist Church memorial.

"Private Reynolds was the only son of Mr and Mrs H Reynolds of Scotland Road, Melksham. He was formerly employed at the Avon India Rubber Works. He was called up in the early part of 1916 and sent to France in June of that year with the Wiltshire regiment. He had

been reported as missing since October 18th last and official information has now been received that he was killed but no details are given of the circumstances or even as to the date of his death. Private Reynolds parents formerly resided in Trowbridge and several relatives are still living in the town."
(Picture and Text courtesy Wiltshire Times)

Wednesday 18th October 1916 War diary extract

The artillery shelled heavily the enemy positions until 2.40am when the bombardment was intense. Previous to this hour C & D coys were formed up in waves, each company having two platoons in the first wave and two in the second wave. Both of these were in advance of the front line . A coy formed the third wave, lying behind the parados of our front line, and B coy were ready to move up from support line. At 3.40am the 21st Brigade attacked, the 2nd Wilts on the left, the 18th Kings L'pools in the centre and the 2nd Yorks on the right, with the 19th Manchester's in support. Very little information forthcoming. Apparently C & D coys reached their objectives but failed to take them. 2/LT EW WARE wounded and missing, 2/LT SG IIINE wounded; LT FN VERRAN and 2/LT DI LYALL missing, all of D company. 2/LT EB GARNETT missing, 2/LT IC TRENCH, VW VENABLES, AEL CRAVEN wounded, all of C coy. A coy advanced but were held up by wire and were eventually driven back. 2/LTS HT Newton and HL REEVES wounded. B coy advanced but lost direction and part of the coy under Capt VH CLAY crossed the SUNKEN ROAD and got into the first German lines. They bombed up a communication trench , but were driven back before a block could be made.
They again bombed up the trench but were again driven back on account with shortage in bombs. On being reinforced by the Cameron's of the 26th Brigade 9th Division this trench was captured and a block made. The first line trench captured in conjunction with the 9th Division, of which we held a part, and was consolidated. Capt VH CLAY was killed during the consolidation, and 2/Lt JH THOMPSON was killed during the advance. 2/Lt EA CARRINGTON volunteered to seek information as regards the position of our companies some while after the attack started. He did not return and parties sent in search afterwards found no trace of him. 2/LT RL SCULLY who acted as liaison officer was buried by a shell and consequently had to be sent down suffering from the shock. Information did not arrive and it was understood that the attack had failed on the whole of the 21st Brigade front but that the 9th Division had gained all their objectives.
Our estimated casualty report read: 14 officers 350 other ranks. The remainder of the Battalion held the old British front line from the SUNKEN ROAD to the junction of TURKLANE and FRONTLINE. The trenches were by this time in an appalling state owing to the bad weather. The 19th Manchester Regt took over the front line from TURKLANE to the right.

 ### 203143 *Private Frederick RICHARDS, 2nd Battalion Duke of Edinburgh's Wiltshire Regiment*

Died of wounds on the 2nd April 1918. Born, resident and enlisted Melksham. He is buried in St Souplet British Cemetery, Nord, France. Plot I. Row G. Grave 35.

(Picture on horseback courtesy of Mr Derek Dyer)

Quiet day. Lieut S COLLIER rejoined from X Corps Signalling School and a few men from leave. Classes of instruction were formed for Lewis Gunners and Signallers. Casualties during the recent action (commencing on 21/3/18) were:- Officers Killed. Capt WB GARDNER, MC. Wounded. Lieut CL USHER, 2/Lieuts K D'O HUSBAND EH CAPP and WGE WILTSHIRE. Missing - Lieut Col AVP MARTIN, Capts AO CLAYTON, LC MAKEHAM and HH MARTYN, Lieuts TW GLYNN and RMP BEAVEN, 2/Lieuts JFF McQUEEN, RH EDWARDS, EW APPS, AR MOORE, P KING-SMITH, WR GOSLING, SS MILLER, EL HALL, CD BAKER, BM IVISON and HJ HULBERT. Other ranks. Killed 4 Wounded 9 missing 597.

55040 *Private Albert Charles RICKETTS, 13th Battalion Welsh Regiment*

Killed in action on the 27th August 1918. He was born in Yeovil, Somerset, enlisted Devizes, resident in Melksham. Brother of William S. Ricketts, of 17, Mudford Rd., Yeovil, Somerset. He has no known grave and is commemorated on the Vis En Artois Memorial, Pas de Calais, France Panel 7. He is also commemorated on the United Reform Church memorial and on the Avon Employees Memorial.

B2/164012 *Gunner Charles Stanley RICKETTS, Royal Field Artillery*

Died in United Kingdom 5th October 1916 aged 34. He was born in Yeovil, Somerset, enlisted Melksham. Husband of Margaret A Ricketts, 19 West End, Melksham, Wiltshire. Buried Portsmouth Milton Cemetery I. 7.58.

WR/178698 Sapper E ROGERS, Royal Engineers

Died 10th March 1919. Aged 53. Husband of Emily Rogers, of 45, Dunch Rd., Melksham. Buried in Shaw Christ Church Graveyard, Melksham Without, Wiltshire. Grave A

2301 Lance Corporal Frederick John SAWYER, 2nd/4th (Territorial Force), Duke of Edinburgh's Wiltshire Regiment

Killed in action in Mesopotamia on the 22nd November 1915. Born and resident Melksham. He has no known grave and is commemorated on the Basra Memorial, Iraq Panels 30 and 64. He is also remembered on the United Reform Church memorial. The following is a transcript of a letter sent to the father of Pte Sawyer from Poona, India, dated the 7th February 1915.

Sir,

I expect you will be surprised to hear from me but as Quartermaster-Sergeant of his company and a friend of your son I thought I would write a few lines to say how deeply we deplore his loss. Personally I feel it as much as if I had lost a brother. I knew him well at Marlborough and since we have served together our friendship has grown and I have had no deeper shock throughout the war than when I heard of his death, and so it was throughout our Company - to a man. They liked him and respected him. He had led an absolutely clean life since he had joined us, and no man had heard a foul word pass his lips. As a soldier he was one of the best, if not the best, L/Corporal in our Regiment. Keen and intelligent and a good athlete, he excelled in all he undertook, and he would have undoubtedly been promoted long ere this had he not so gallantly volunteered to serve his Country in the Gulf. I hardly like to tell you of the way he met his death, but I feel that I must, for it was one of the most heroic acts in that dreadful engagement. A Col-Sergt had been badly wounded, and Fred was bandaging his wound with his field bandages. As he was doing so a bullet struck him in the left forearm, almost severing the arm but still he kept on with his act of mercy, another bullet struck him in the thigh, but utterly disregarding his wounds he tried to complete the task but another bullet struck him in the stomach and he dropped. His comrades covered him and a Sergt of ours with overcoats and endeavoured to find an ambulance; in the confusion it was hours before it reached them and when it arrived they had both gone to their rest. So died a true hero. I hope God, in his mercy, will give you strength to bear up under your trouble. From what I know of Fred, there was no way in which he would sooner have died than in defence of his country.

By army regulations his kit was sold at Poona early in last week, and realised Rs 55-4-0 = in English money £3-19-0. This has been transferred to your son's account in the Oxford and Bucks L.I. Regiment and it will eventually reach you. I am enclosing Fred's letter and a pocket testament which we took from his kit. If you can spare time I should be glad of a line to say that they reached you.

My Company Sergt-Major and I join in tendering you our deepest sympathy in your great loss.

I beg to remain, Sir,

Yours sincerely,

A.R. Wyatt. Coy. Q.M.S.

'C' Company,

2/4th Wiltshire Regiment.

(Transcript courtesy of Mr Richard Staniforth)

 ### 1131 Corporal Walter SCARLETT, 2nd Battalion Leinster Regiment

Killed in action on the 7th May 1916 aged 35 years. Husband of Florence Mary Scarlett of Beanacre, Melksham, Wiltshire. He is buried at Ration Farm, La Plus Douve Annexe, Grave ref II.C. 7. Formerly 13254 Wiltshire Regiment

The 2nd Leinster's were part of the 73rd Brigade and in April 1916 they were in the line in front of Messines which was quiet. On 29/30 April there was a gas attack by the Germans followed by an assault. The purpose of the raid was to destroy a mine shaft being prepared by North Staffordshire's of 72nd Bde. The 2nd Leinster's suffered 55 casualties of which 19 were gassed and less than half a dozen killed. This was a new type of gas and some men died who had been affected and took exercise within 24 hours of the attack.

M/10909 Engine Room Artificer 3rd Class Frederick William SHADWELL, H.M.S. Glatton, Royal Navy.

Killed on the 16th September 1918 after an explosion on board ship, he is buried in Gillingham Woodlands Cemetery 15.804-6.

"Frederick William Shadwell was the eldest son of Mr and Mrs F.G. Shadwell of Church Walk Melksham. He was 26 years of age and had served in the Royal Navy for almost four years. Formerly he was in the employ of Messrs Spencer and Co, engineers and was one of the first to volunteer for naval service after the outbreak of war. He was well known and very popular in Melksham having for some time been a regular player in the Town Football Club. He served for some years as a member of the Church Lads Brigade and was also in the Parish Church Choir. Much sympathy is felt for his parents whose younger son is also in the navy. Another brother was accidentally drowned whilst bathing some years ago in Melksham."
(Picture and text courtesy of Wiltshire Times)

Shortly after arriving at Dover, having taken on ammunition elsewhere, there was an accidental explosion in the 6" magazine that soon threatened to spread to the 9.2" magazines - if this had happened the resulting explosion would have devastated much of the port area. Crews were sent onboard to aid the existing crew in trying to contain the blaze and, when this proved impossible, to open the sea cocks to flood the magazines. Unfortunately this wasn't totally successful and Vice Admiral Roger Keyes gave the order to have HMS Glatton torpedoed to avert the imminent catastrophe. There wasn't time to remove many of the sailors who were still struggling valiantly at their task, and they perished when Glatton was sunk. The wreck remained in Dover Harbour until the 1920's, when it was salvaged and the bodies finally recovered - they were transported to Chatham for identification and then interred in Woodlands Cemetery, Gillingham.

28855 Acting 2nd Corporal Harry SHARPE, 25th AT Company Royal Engineers

Died on the 11th November 1917 aged 27. Born and resident in Melksham, enlisted in Bath. Son of Emily Sharp, Semington Rd. Melksham. He is buried in Anzin St Aubine British Cemetery, Pas de Calais, France. Plot III. Row A. Grave 1. Also remembered on the United Reform Church Memorial

10926 Corporal Albert SHEPPARD, 2nd Battalion Duke of Edinburgh's Wiltshire Regiment

Killed in action on the 15th February 1916. Born and resident Melksham, enlisted Devizes. He is buried in Carnoy Military Cemetery, Somme, France. Plot/Row/Section T. Grave 9. Also remembered on the United Reform Church Memorial

Extract from Battalion War Diary, Tuesday 15th Feb
The day was very quiet. The weather was very bad.

33206 Private George SHEPPARD, 2nd Battalion Duke of Edinburgh's Wiltshire Regiment

Died of wounds on the 14th April 1917. Born and resident in Melksham, enlisted in Warminster. He is buried in Warlencourt Halte British Cemetery, Saulty, Pas de Calais, France. Plot VII. Row F. Grave 6. Also remembered on the United Reform Church Memorial

58015 Private Fred SKUSE, 9th Infantry Labour Company, Devonshire Regiment

Died 30th March 1917 aged 34. Born Beamore, enlisted Melksham. Son of Cornelius and Elizabeth Skuse; husband of Emily Alice Skuse, of Lower Stanton Farm, Stanton St. Quinton, Chippenham. Native of Beanacre, Melksham. He is buried in Etaples Military Cemetery, Pas de Calais, France. Plot XXII. Row D. Grave 13A

63794 Sergeant Reginald Charles SNOOK, 24th Battery Royal Field Artillery

Killed in action on the 16th July 1915 aged 24. Born in Devizes, enlisted Melksham. Son of Frederick and Kate Snook, of Shurnhold, Melksham, Wilts. He is buried in Potijze Burial Ground Cemetery, Ypres, West-Vlaanderen, Belgium AI. Grave 8. Also remembered in Shaw Church and Old Broughton Road Baptist Church.

28854 Sapper William Frederick SPENCER, 57th Field Company Royal Engineers

Killed in action on the 24th March 1917. He was born in Melksham and enlisted in Bath. He is buried in St Vaast Post Military Cemetery Richebourge-L'Avoue, Pas de Calais, France. Plot IV. Row E. Grave 7. Also remembered on the United Reform Church Memorial

"The death of another well known and highly esteemed Melksham resident has occurred on the battlefield in France, the deceased being Sapper William Spencer, R.E. The sad news was received by the family on Wednesday morning by a letter dated 24th March.
"It is with the deepest regret that I write to inform you that your son was killed in action this morning at about 9 a.m.. Military regulations prevent me from giving you minute details of this tragic occurrence but I think I may be permitted to say that it was caused by shell fire and death was practically instantaneous. Your son had been on detachment and had only returned to the company about a fortnight, so that although I have been with the company for six months I knew little of him. I know however from my sergeant and the men of the section that he was an industrious and painstaking sapper and was highly esteemed by all who knew him. I have arranged for a Nonconformist chaplain to perform the last rites tomorrow (Sunday); he will be buried in a British Cemetery. I will write again and inform you of the proceedings. In conclusion I wish to convey to you and yours my heartfelt sympathy and I trust you will be given strength to bear this sudden blow."
Sincerely yours
EDWARD FINCHAM
Lieut R.E.

"Sapper Spencer who was 27 years of age was the youngest son of the late Mr Frederick Spencer of Union Street and before the war was a moulder in the employ of Messrs Spencer & Co engineers. He was popular with all classes being much esteemed both by the firm and his fellow workers. As a boy he appeared to be rather under than over the average in stature and stamina, but to use a common phrase he "had a good head on his shoulders" and made the best of his opportunities for physical culture etc. As a result he developed a fine athletic frame and showed prowess in various manly games, one of his chief acquirements being the art of wrestling. It was not long before he entered the Army that he gave an exhibition at the Picture Hall where he successfully wrestled with champions from Bristol and elsewhere, to the delight of a crowded audience.

Just after the breaking out of hostilities Mr Spencer volunteered his services for the Army joining the Royal Engineers and for two years he was in France. During the greater part of the time he was engaged in touch work in connection with the erection of fencing for the British troops, destroying that of the Germans etc. Although frequently in great danger he met with no injury beyond a very slight wound – practically a bruise on one of his shoulders. He was afterwards given a rest, i.e. was set to work on less arduous and dangerous business. Recently, however, as intimated in the officer's letter, he returned to his company.

We are sure his many friends will share the regret expressed by the officer at his decease, and sympathise with the family in their bereavement. Deceased has a brother, Sapper H. Spencer also in the R.E. in France and one employed in a munitions factory in England."

(Picture and text courtesy of Wiltshire Times)

320417 Private Frederick Percy SYDEE, Royal Wiltshire Yeomanry

Died on the 20th June 1918. He is buried in south end of new part of Melksham Church Cemetery, Melksham, Wiltshire. Also remembered on the Avon employees memorial and Old Broughton Road Baptist Church.

"Private Sydee passed away at the Cambridge Military Hospital Aldershot he was the fourth son of Mr W.S. Sydee of Beanacre Road Melksham. He was 25 years of age and was previously employed at the Avon Rubber Works. In September 1914 he joined the R.W.Y. and subsequently saw service in France for over a year, being attached to the 3rd Reserve Regiment of Hussars. While there he

contracted pleurisy and in August 1917 was sent back to England, but although he made temporary improvement he was able to return home but he never recovered. The body was conveyed to Melksham where the funeral was conducted with full military honours. Pte Sydee comes of a well known and highly respected family. Two brothers are now serving with the colours, one in India with the Wilts and one in the Canadian Flying Corps."
(Picture and text courtesy of the Wiltshire Times)

70622 Private Herbert TAYLOR, 144th Company Machine Gun Corps

Killed in action on the 16th August 1917. He was born and enlisted in Devizes, but was resident in Melksham. Formerly 5193, Worcestershire Regiment. He has no known grave and is commemorated on Tyne Cot Memorial, Zonnebeke, West-Vlaanderen, Belgium Panels 154 to 159 and 163A

SS/1618 Leading Seaman Andrew TRIMMING, RFR/PO/B/4558 SS Kohinur, Royal Navy

He was Killed in Action on the 25th May 1917. On 25th May 1917 the HMT Kohinur, which was built in 1905, was torpedoed by U 38, 150 miles N from Alexandria, Egypt, in the Mediterranean Sea. The ship was travelling from Salonika to Karachi, 37 lives were lost. He is commemorated on the Portsmouth Memorial ref 24.

2116 Private William TRUEMAN, 7th Battalion Prince Albert's Somerset Light Infantry

Killed in Action on the 30th November 1917. He was born in Seend and enlisted in Trowbridge, resident Melksham. Formerly 3543, Wiltshire Regiment. He has no known grave and is commemorated on Cambrai Memorial, Louverval, Nord, France Panels 4 and 5.

Lieutenant Raymond George VINCENT, 73rd Battalion Canadian Infantry

Husband of Violet Vincent, of Prospect House, Trowbridge, Wilts, England. Died on 29th March 1917 aged 30 years. He is buried in Barlin Communal Cemetery Extension ref I.J.51

 1171 Corporal William Henry WALKER, Worcestershire Regiment

William was born in Lacock in 1891 his father was Henry and his mother was Sarah Jane Walker. He enlisted in the Worcestershire Regiment on 28th June 1908. He was discharged on 28th July 1918 as unfit for action. During he service in the Great War Will saw active service in Egypt and France He married Amelia Frances Ricketts (formerly Walker), of 6, Leaze Rd., The Forest, Melksham in 1916 and they had one daughter Millicent Mary Walker born in 1916. Sadly after his discharge he was not a well man and was taken into Devizes Wiltshire County Asylum on 2nd Oct 1918. William died the very next day on 3rd October 1918, aged 27 of an abscess on his kidneys. He was laid to rest in the south end of new part of Melksham Church Cemetery, Melksham, Wiltshire.

William Henry Walker

Pictures courtesy Mr & Mrs Heard from Bradford on Avon

48289 Private Percy Louis WHITING, 3rd Battalion Duke of Edinburgh's Wiltshire Regiment

Died 24th November 1918. Aged 24. Husband of E. M. M. Whiting, of 4, Canon Square, Melksham. Buried in south end of new part of Melksham Church Cemetery, Melksham, Wiltshire.
*Listed on the Memorial as PC Whiting

"Pte Percy Louis Whiting, 3rd Wiltshire Regiment, died from septic pneumonia at Elsford Military Hospital, on Sunday November 24th at the early age of 24. He joined the Army on August 1st last, being previously in business as a hairdresser at Mersen near Colchester. He recently fell victim to the common complaint and did not recover. He leaves a widow (daughter of Mr and Mrs G Marks of Canon Square, Melksham) and one child, about six months old.
The body was brought to Melksham where the interment took place on Friday. The service was held in the Congregational Church, the Rev W.J. Farr officiating. Full military honours were accorded, a firing party of 10 being provided by the local Volunteer Corps, and the "Last Post" was sounded by an Australian soldier. Among those present were a number of men from the Red Cross Hospitals."
(Text courtesy of Wiltshire Times)

10966 Private Charles Frederick WILLIAMS, 1st Battalion Duke of Edinburgh's Wiltshire Regiment

Died of wounds on the 22nd June 1915 aged 17. Born and resident in Melksham, he enlisted in Devizes. Son of Frederick Charles and Mary Ann Williams, of 5, Market Place, Melksham. He is commemorated on Ypres Menin Gate Memorial, Ypres, West-Vlaanderen Belgium Panel 53. Also remembered on the Avon Employees Memorial.

Extract from Battalion War Diary Tuesday 22nd June 1915

Fine and hot. A Coy took up position in HOOGE trenches. 2 platoon in C1 and C trench from tunnel to ISLAND POST. B Coy in trenches N of ZOUVE Wood to support A Coy. Bombardment took place 7.30 - 8p.m. At 8p.m. No 1 & 3 platoons attacked but were held up by Machine gun fire. The two officers leading attack were shot and the men returned to our fire trenches. The action was broken off. The German parapets appeared to be little damaged. Casualties. 2nd Lieut A N Mclean killed. 2nd Lieuts A C W Broadhurst and N L Carrington wounded. Other ranks, 24. About midnight the Battn was relieved and returned to billets near VLAMERTINGE.

18944 Private Albert Charles (Bertie) WOOTTEN, 6th Battalion Wiltshire Regiment

Died 05/11/1916 Aged 19 Son of Sidney and Ellen Elizabeth Wootten, of Yew Cottage, Sandridge Lane, Bromham, Wilts. He has no known grave and is commemorated on the Theipval Memorial Pier and Face 13A. Also remembered on the Avon Employees memorial.

"Pte Albert Charles Wootten second son of Mr and Mrs Sidney Wootten, whose eldest son is also serving in India, was like his comrade Boulter only 19 when he made the supreme sacrifice for King and country on November 5th last while fighting in France. He Belonged to the Wilts Regiment."
(Picture and text courtesy Wiltshire Times)

7048 Lance Sergeant D.F. WORSDELL, 2nd Battalion Duke of Edinburgh's Wiltshire Regiment

Killed in action on the 25th September 1915. He has no known grave and is commemorated on the Loos Memorial Panel 102. *Appears on the memorial as DJ Worsdell

Extract from Battalion War Diary Saturday 25th September 1915

Battn moved at 12.30am marched via LA BOURSE and SAILLY, arriving at a reserve line of trenches SE of NOYELLES at point L12 o 6.6 at about 3am. Bombardment becomes intense. At about 6am the attack was launched. Battn ordered to advance through VERMELLES up communication trench (CHAPEL ALLEY) to occupy front line at point G11 o 9.8. Capt King wounded. 2/Lt FH Friend assumed command of 'A' Coy. Following the advance of the 20th Brigade the Battalion occupies the front and support German lines. Lt Col BH Leatham DSO then gave orders for the Battn to advance in open order in direction of CITE ST ELIE keeping to the north of HULLUCH ROAD, our right flank connecting with the 2nd Bedfordshire's left. The Battn advanced in the following order, 'B' Coy on the left Capt WM GEDDES in command, 'A' Coy on right 2/Lt FH Friend in command, two platoons of each comp leading, two platoons behind, 'C' Coy in support, 'D' Coy in reserve, Major RMP Gillson in command of 'C' Coy, Capt EC Mudge in command of 'D' Coy, the whole were led by Major CG Forsyth, and experiencing extremely heavy rifle and machine gun fire from the front came to a line held very weakly by a

mixture of 8th Devon & 2nd Borders. The trench contained 4 German field guns and ammunition. Our losses were heavy and included the following Officers
casualties Capt GMU Wilson, 2/Lts CFB Hodgins JH Clarke WHG Durrant killed. Major RMP Gillson, 2nd Lt FH Friend wounded the latter seriously.
At dusk the Battn was relieved by the 9/Devonshire Regt and took up a new front at BRESLAU AVENUE our right resting on the latter Regiment.

Captain George Richard WYLD, 3rd Battalion Wiltshire Regiment. Attached 1st Battalion Berkshire Regiment

Died 24th December 1914. Aged 37. Only son of Edwin George Wyld, Vicar of Melksham, Wilts, and of Mary Caroline Wyld, eldest daughter of Sir Hungerford Pollen, 3rd Baronet. He was born at Woodborough, Wilts on the 8th July 1879.

George R. Wyld.

Educated Marlborough and on leaving there entered the Stock Exchange. Saw active service in the South African Campaign 1899 – 1902 with the 13th Middlesex V.R.C (now the Queen's Westminster's). He was awarded Queens South Africa Medal with four clasps. He was appointed a Hon Lieutenant on 1st July 1901. When the Great War broke out he was on the Reserve of Officers and immediately volunteered for foreign service. He was attached to the Kings Royal Rifle Corp on 19th Aug 1914 and was gazetted as a Captain in the 3rd Wiltshire Regiment on 7th Oct 1914. On the 1st December 1914 he was attached to the 1st Battalion Berkshire Regiment from the 2nd Battalion. He was with the 7th Division and was Killed in Action at Givenchy on 24th Dec 1914. The Chaplain wrote "He was most popular with his brother officers of the Berkshire Regiment and was considered very efficient in his duty, and it was whilst bravely doing his duty in a trench at Givenchy that he was mortally wounded by a bullet" He is buried in Brown's Road Military Cemetery, Festubert, Pas de Calais, France. PlotV. Row A. Grave 6

Extract from Battalion War Diary Thursday 24th December 1914
A hard frost last night. A very quiet day. Captain Wyld killed near support trenches from stray bullet after midnight

Extract from Battalion War Diary Friday 25th December 1914
In morning Commanding Officer went round trenches and distributed Kings and Queens Xmas card, which was much appreciated. Sapped into a German communications trench. GOC 2nd Division sent congratulatory message on work done by the battalion. C&D Coys relieved A&B in trenches. Buried Capt Wyld in garden of house near Pont FIXE.

Brewer brothers remembered with their parents in Melksham Churchyard

George Crook remembered in Melksham Churchyard

Pte Dodimead remembered in Melksham Churchyard

Frank Burbidge remembered with his parents in Melksham Churchyard

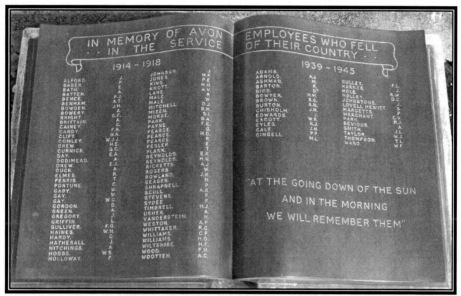

Avon employees memorial from both wars

To the relatives of every soldier who died a death plaque was issued. Due to its resemblance to a penny coin it was more commonly known as the 'Dead Mans Penny'. The Medal group was commonly known as the 'Pip, Squeak & Wilfred'. There are two variations of the Star medal the first was the 1914 star which was issued to the men who saw active service during 1914. The 14-15 Star was presented to soldiers who had served in the front line during 1915. Those who first saw active after 1915 were not awarded the Star medal. The middle medal was the British War Medal and the one on the right is the Victory Medal. Those who arrived in theatre from 1916 onwards would have only received the British War Medal and the Victory Medal. Should a soldier have been wounded and was unable to serve any longer and he was discharged back to civilian life, he would have been issued with a Silver War Badge which he would have worn on his civilian clothing to signify that he had served.

Silver War Badge

The following all have a Melksham Connection but are not commemorated on the local memorial

12914 Lance Corporal Victor Wallace ALFORD, 'B' Company 1st Battalion Duke of Edinburgh's Wiltshire Regiment

Killed in action on the 1st October 1918 aged 25 years. Son of Mr and Mrs G Alford of The Gravel, Holt, Wiltshire. Born in Melksham he enlisted in Bradford on Avon. He is buried in Le Cateau Military Cemetery I.B.150

SS/2011 Able Seaman Alfred Henry ALEXANDER, H.M.T.B. 82 Royal Navy

"Alfred died in Portland Naval Hospital from the effects of influenza on December 8th 1918 and was buried in Broughton Gifford Cemetery Nr Melksham. He had joined the navy in 1908 and saw service around the world. At the time of his death he was serving on a Torpedo Boat. It is sad that after undergoing all the hardships of the war he should have died within sight of peace, and his death has an added pathos from the fact that the was married to Winifred Nellie Alexander, of 22, Vicarage Rd., Whitehall, Bristol only a few months ago. He was a man of a singular winning and sunny personality, which made him always a favourite and his death is much regretted by all who knew him. Below is copy of a letter received by his widow.

"Dear Mrs Alexander,
Please accept the deepest sympathy from the officers and crew of T.B. 82. Your husband was a great favourite with all aboard and his absence will be greatly felt by us, more especially as in a small boat like this the officers are brought in to very close contact with the crew and I was enabled to see what a fine shipmate he was. If there is any possible way I can help you I shall be only too pleased to do so.

I am, yours faithfully
R.W. TAYLOR Commanding Officer"
(Portrait picture and text courtesy Wiltshire Times)

775006 Sergeant Percy Albert Gregory ALLEN, 'B' Battery 310th Brigade Royal Field Artillery

Killed in action on the 19th April 1917 aged 35. Son of John and Annie Allen, of Melksham, Wilts; husband of Annie Allen, of 28, Bridge St., Llandaff, Cardiff. Buried in St Sever Cemetery Extension, Rouen O. IX. F. 7.

15393 Gunner A ASH, 6th Ammunition Col Royal Field Artillery

Killed in action on the 30th August 1916 aged 33. Son of Levi Mortimer, of Norrington Gate Farm, Broughton Gifford, Melksham, Wilts, and the late Emily Mortimer. Buried in Baghdad North Gate War Cemetery XXI. A. 16.

28540 Private Reginald ASH, 15th Service Battalion Hampshire Regiment

Killed in action on the 2nd October 1918 aged 19. Son of Mr. and Mrs. E. J. Ash, of Broughton Gifford, Melksham, Wilts. Enlisted in Trowbridge. He has no known grave and is commemorated on the Tyne Cot Memorial Panels 88 to and 162.

"Private Ash joined the Dorset's in March 1917 at the age of 18. Later he was attached to the Hants and prior to his death had been on active service in France for several months. He was the youngest of six sons four of whom are in the Army. Private Ash was in the employ of Messrs Spencer and Co Melksham. He was connected with the local Wesleyan Church and was a scholar in the Sunday school from very early days until his country called him to sterner duties. He was very highly regarded by all who knew him and he is mourned not only by his family, the church and Sunday School but also by the village generally."
(Picture and text courtesy Wiltshire Times)

26040 Sergeant Frederick ASHBEE, 126ᵗʰ Siege Battery Royal Garrison Artillery

Died of wounds on the 7ᵗʰ August 1917. He was born in Billericay, Essex and when he enlisted he was living in Gosport Hampshire. Husband of Alice E. Ashbee, of Seend Cleeve, Melksham, Wilts. He is buried in Meninghem Military Cemetery IV.A.38

Major Charles Selwyn AWDRY D.S.O. Royal Wiltshire Yeomanry attached 6ᵗʰ Battalion Wiltshire Regiment

Killed in Action on the 24ᵗʰ March 1918. He has no known grave and is commemorated on Panel 6 at the Pozieres Memorial.

Charles was born on the 23ʳᵈ March 1877 son of C Awdry. He attended Waynflete School before attending Winchester. On the outbreak of the South African war he went to the Cape with the Imperial Yeomanry where he saw active service and was Mentioned in Despatches. In 1904 he became a partner in the firm W.H. Smith & Son. Charles, held a commission in the Royal Wiltshire Yeomanry and in 1917 he was given command of the 6ᵗʰ Battalion Wiltshire Regiment. During his tenure as their commanding officer he was awarded the Distinguished Service Order (D.S.O.) and was twice mentioned in despatches.

During March 1918 the Wiltshire's were heavily involved in action against the Germans and on the 25ᵗʰ March Charles was reported missing and it is presumed that he died on this day. He was married to Miss Constance Lilias Basteson, of Heston, Middlesex and was a Justice of the Peace for the County of Wiltshire. They had five children; Charles Edwin Awdry b 1906, Selwyn Ambrose Awdry b 1908, Henry Godwin Awdry b 1911, Ambrose Leonard Awdry b 1913 & Lilias Margaret Awdry b 1916. Charles was a keen sportsman and represented Wiltshire at cricket from 1895 to 1915. He also played for Lords and as such is commemorated on their Roll of Honour.

His DSO Citation (London Gazette No31043, 2 December 1918).

Maj. Charles Selwyn Awdry, R. Wilts. Yeomanry attached to the 6th Battalion Wiltshire Regiment.

For conspicuous gallantry and devotion to duty. He showed the greatest coolness and contempt of danger in conducting the retirement of the remnants of his battalion, and though greatly exhausted organised a new line of defence during the night. Next day, by his fine example he did much to steady the men of many scattered units.

Winchester XI in 1896 CS Awdry 2nd from right on back row

 13958 Corporal Charles BAGWELL, 10th Battalion Devonshire Regiment

Killed in action on the 24th April 1917 aged 21 years. Son of John Bagwell of Shepton Montague, Castle Cary, Somerset. Born in Melksham he enlisted in Taunton. He has no known grave and is commemorated on the Doiran Memorial in Salonika.

 7718 Private Clifford Nelson BAILEY, 1st Battalion Duke of Edinburgh's Wiltshire Regiment.

Killed in action on the 30th October 1914. He was born in Melksham but at the time of his enlistment was living in Trowbridge. He is buried in the Ypres Town Cemetery Extension II.A.22.

18771 Private Victor BAKER, 7th Battalion Duke of Edinburgh's Wiltshire Regiment.

Killed in action between the dates 16th & 18th October 1918. He was born in Melksham and at the time of his call up he was living in Trowbridge. He is buried in the Pommereuil British Cemetery D.61.

18307 Lance Corporal Henry George BARTHOLOMEW, 1st Battalion Duke of Edinburgh's Wiltshire Regiment

Killed in action on the 16th June 1915 aged 19. Son of Percival and Fanny Bartholomew, of Neston Lodge, Bath Rd Atworth, Melksham. He has no known grave and is commemorated on the Ypres Menin Gate Memorial Panel 53.

Extract of Battalion War Diary Wednesday 16th June 1915

2.50a.m. Our artillery commenced bombardment on German trenches situated between ROULERS railway and Southern end of Ypres Wood.
4.20a.m. The 9th Bde had carried the first line of German trenches and 1 platoon of C Coy assaulted trench at S end of Ypres Wood which was taken
without difficulty. A bombing party started to work up the enemy's trench in the direction of HOOGE and made rapid progress. The remainder of C Coy & D Coy followed up. The leading men (5a.m.) reached a point some 100yds from HOOGE village; meanwhile a Communication Trench was dug from culvert under Menen Road to S end of Ypres Wood and endeavours made to join up two pieces of German trench running E towards HOOGE. Until 6a.m. the situation remained unchanged.
6a.m. More progress towards HOOGE was made - a point within 50yds of the village being reached in the German trench. Between 6a.m. and 9a.m. the situation remained unchanged. Work of barricading and reversing the parapets was continued.
9a.m. The Germans advanced down two CTs from the N and under cover of a heavy fire started bombing heavily. We replied with grenades, this exchange lasted about 1 and a half hours.
10.30a.m. Our supply of grenades became exhausted and the Germans succeeded in driving us slowly back down the trench. In retiring we suffered heavy casualties during the period of the action.
11a.m. We evacuated the eastern portion of the German trench . We retired in the open and lost a considerable number of men in doing so. A counter charge was organised about this time to check the enemy's advance, but without success, as the officer and many men were shot down and the remainder made no progress.
3p.m. Germans commenced a heavy bombardment of Ypres Wood and the trenches which had been captured in the morning. Our guns replied by shelling the German's about BELLEWARDE Lake, presumably to break up any attempt at counter attack. The situation remained unchanged in our trenches.
6.30p.m. Germans started a very heavy bombardment of Ypres Wood which lasted about 1 hour.
8p.m. Germans fired a considerable number of gas shells in the neighbourhood of the Menen Road but these only caused temporary inconvenience.
11p.m. Suffolk's started digging trench parallel to C trench from corner of Ypres Wood to culvert. The trench running eastwards from the corner of Ypres Wood was abandoned and blocked over a distance of 30yds.

3626 Private Henry James BETHELL, 4th Battalion Duke of Edinburgh's Wiltshire Regiment

Son of Henry Bethell, of Trowbridge; husband of Ruth B. Bethell, of Slades Farm, Whitley, Melksham. He died at home on the 7th March 1916 he is buried in Trowbridge Cemetery ref P.2.2532.

 ### 114541 Private Wilfrid Ewart BIGWOOD 'A' Company 1st Battalion Canadian Mounted Rifles

Killed in action on the 5th June 1916. Son of Lewin John and Emily Maria Bigwood, of "Formosa," The Spa. Melksham, Wilts, England. He has no known grave and is commemorated on the Ypres Menin Gate Memorial Panels 30, 32. Also Remembered on the United Reform Church Memorial.

 ### 30309 Private Cecil John BODMAN, 5th Battalion South Wales Borderers.

Killed in action on the 30th May 1918 aged 20 years. Son of Edwin and Emma Bodman of 64, Pochin Crescent, Tredegar, Monmouthshire. He was born in Melksham and enlisted in Tredegar. He is buried in the Chambrecy British Cemetery VI.C.2.

T3/025621 Driver Arthur Rowland BROWN, Army Service Corps

Enlisted Trowbridge resident in Melksham. Son of James and Louisa Brown, of New Buildings, Atworth. Died Home on the 6th June 1917 he is buried in the Atworth Congregational Chapel yard.

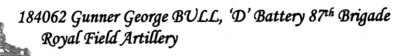

184062 Gunner George BULL, 'D' Battery 87th Brigade Royal Field Artillery

Died of Wounds 16/02/1918. He enlisted in Trowbridge and was resident in Melksham prior to his call up. He is buried in Rocquigny-Equancourt Road, British Cemetery, Manancourt IX.F.27

"Gunner George Bull was a native of Broughton Gifford and was 34 years of age. He was called to the colours in 1916 and went to the Front in March 1917. He was looking forward to leave this month. He was a member of the church choir for over 18 years and possessed an excellent voice.

His services were in request for many local entertainments and those he ungrudgingly gave.
He had helped in entertainments in the Melksham Liberal Club, at Atworth for the Red Cross, as well as in his native village. For many years he worked for EA Gore and Co. He will be much missed."
(Picture and text courtesy of Wiltshire Times)

M/321806 Private John Harold BURBIDGE. 1018th MT Company Royal Army Service Corps

Killed in action on the 19th September 1918 aged 38. Son of Thomas and Louisa Burbidge of Melksham. Husband of Annie Mary Burbidge of 5 Colne Road, Lexden, Colchester. Buried in the Tehran War Cemetery, Iran III.A.3

10010 Private Thomas BURBIDGE, 1st Battalion Coldstream Guards.

Killed in action on the 15th September 1916. At the time of his call up he was living at Seend Stocks, Nr Melksham, Wiltshire. He has no known grave and is commemorated on the Thiepval Memorial Pier and Face 7 D and 8 D.

204640 Corporal George CAINEY, 1st Battalion Duke of Edinburgh's Wiltshire Regiment

Killed in action on the 27th May 1918. He was born in South Wraxall, enlisted in Bradford on Avon and was resident in Melksham when he was called up for duty. Husband of Olive Turtle (formerly Cairey), of Purlpit, Atworth, Melksham, Wilts. He has no known grave and is commemorated on the Soissons Memorial.

Extract from War Diary 27th May 1918 – Guyencourt France

1a.m. enemy starts a heavy gas bombardment which lasts until 5a.m. when he commenced to attack the forward Battn line held by the 8th Div.
7.30a.m. Orders received to move forward to cover retirement of front line troops and Capt Priestley with 3 Coys takes up position further forward.
10.15a.m. Battn again moves forward an holds line in front of BOUFFIGNEREUX.
11.30a.m. - 3.30p.m. Line held as follows, D left Coy, C B A 1 platoon of C Coy only under 2nd Lieut Parkin [?] in front line, remaining 2 platoons of C support D. Enemy shelling constantly Battn HQ, M Gun fire continually sweeping roads and tracks to HQ and front line. Supplies of SAA were however maintained.
4.15p.m. Capts Priestley & Arnott report situation to CO at Battn HQ.
Capt Priestley wounded, still remains at duty.
5.30p.m. Enemy attacked when owing to greatly superior forces the Battn was compelled to retire

and splitting up into small parties slowly withdrew, fighting rearguard actions. Lieut Col Furze DSO, MC, was killed, a like Capt Brooke RAMC. Capts Arnott & Priestley both believed to wounded and prisoners. Lieuts Sames, H Reid, E Duley [?] were wounded and evacuated , also 2nd Lieuts H Anderson & A M Reid. The 7th Inf Bde came under orders of the 8th Div. Odd detachments were re-organised and sent on to keep the line intact.

 ### 1426 Private Harold Fletcher CAMPBELL, 14th Battalion London Regiment London Scottish

Son of John and Agnes Burns Campbell, of "Isleford," 152, Rock Avenue, Gillingham, Kent. Born at Melksham, Wilts. Died on the 12th February 1917 aged 24 years. He buried in Acton Cemetery ref C.C.7.

Private Campbell's inscription and the memorial in Acton Cemetery
(Pictures courtesy of Mrs Judy Rieck)

 ### 265678 Private Frank Reginald CANDY, 7th Battalion Somerset Light Infantry

Killed in action on the 14th August 1917 aged 25. Husband of Maud E. Kaynes (formerly Candy), of 1, Box Cottage, Whitley, Melksham, Wilts. He is buried in Duhallow ADS Cemetery ref VII.C.2.

 ### 9766 Private F.G. CHANDLER, 2nd Battalion Coldstream Guards

Killed in action on the 19th May 1916 aged 21. Son of William Henry and Emily Jane Chandler, of Martinsade, Seend, Melksham, Wilts. He is buried in Essex Farm Cemetery ref I.A.41.

8755 Private William Joseph CHIVERS, 1st Battalion Duke of Edinburgh's Wiltshire Regiment

Killed in action on the 16th June 1915. He was born in Whitley and living in Melksham. He has no known grave and is commemorated on the Ypres Menin Gate Memorial Panel 53.

"News has been received which places beyond doubt the fact that Private W Chivers, eldest son of Mr and Mrs J Chivers, of Littleworth, Whitley, has given his life for King and Country, and the sympathies of all will go out to the bereaved parents.

Private Chivers was serving with the 2nd Wilts Regiment at Gibraltar on the outbreak of war. He came home with them and went to the front with his battalion. Subsequently he was drafted to the 1st Wilts and served with them for ten months without receiving even a scratch. After an engagement he was reported wounded and missing on June 16 and none of his friends had heard any tidings of him until recently when the sad news was received through the Red Cross Society that while a company of the regiment were digging through an old trench his body was found with bullet wounds in it. This has been confirmed by a letter to the parents from one of his comrades.

Mr and Mrs Chivers ask us to thank all their kind friends for the sympathy expressed for them in the loss of a highly respected and popular son."
(Picture courtesy of Mr and Mrs G Mattock) (Text courtesy of Wiltshire Times)

291753 Private Walter Samuel CLARK, 2nd Battalion Devonshire Regiment

Killed in Action on the 25th November 1917 aged 23. Son of the late Samuel Clark, of 1, West View, Whitley, Melksham; husband of Mabel Clark, of 18, Scotland Rd., Melksham, Wilts. He has no known grave and is commemorated on the Tyne Cot Memorial Panel 38 to 40

9567 Private Reginald Arthur COLES, 1st Battalion Duke of Edinburgh's Wiltshire Regiment.

Killed in action on the 24th April 1916 aged 21 years. He was born in Yeovil but was living in Melksham at the time of his enlistment. Son of Albert Charles and Mary Ellen Coles of Fairfield Farm, Bradford on Avon. He is buried in the Ecoivers Military Cemetery, Mont St Eloi I.F.9

10276 Private William COLLINS, 1st Battalion Duke of Edinburgh's Wiltshire Regiment

Killed in action of the 28th February 1915. William was born in Dorchester and was living in Melksham at the time of his enlistment. He is buried in Kemmel Chateau Military Cemetery G.27

306649 Private William John COOK, 1st/8th Battalion Royal Warwickshire Regiment

Killed in action on the 2nd November 1918 aged 35. Son of Edward and Martha Cook, of Seend, Melksham. Husband of Selina (Grace) Cook, of "Willow Dale," Seend, Melksham, Wilts. He is buried in Pommereuil British Cemetery ref B.54

18149 Private Bernard Newman COTTLE, 1st Battalion Duke of Edinburgh's Wilshire Regiment

Killed in action on the 24th March 1918 aged 19 years. Son of K.M. Cottle of 121 Mortimer St Trowbridge, Wiltshire and the late William Cottle. He was born in Melksham and prior to enlisting in Devizes he was residing in Trowbridge. He has no known grave and is commemorated on the Arras Memorial Bay 7.

201990 Private Cecil CROOK, 1st/4th Battalion Hampshire Regiment

Killed in action on the 23rd February 1917 aged 19. Son of James and Martha Crook, of Shaw Hill, Melksham, Wilts. Formerly 3392 in the Wiltshire Regiment. He has no known grave and is commemorated on the Basra Memorial panels 21 and 63.

8138 Lance Corporal Frederick Albert DEVONISH, 'C' Company 2nd Battalion Essex Regiment

Son of Frederick and Alice Devonish; husband of Mary Brown (formerly Devonish), of 19, New Broughton Rd., Melksham, Wilts. Born at Sandon, Essex. Died on 3rd May 1916 and is buried in Great Baddow St Mary Churchyard ref 188.

(Picture courtesy of Mr Bill Oliver)

8173 Private William Frederick DIFFELL, 2nd Battalion Duke of Edinburgh's Wiltshire Regiment.

Died of Wounds whilst a Prisoner of War on the 29th March 1915. William was born in Melksham and prior to enlisting in Devizes he was living in Corsham. He is buried in the Niederzwehren Cemetery, Kassel, Hessen Germany VII.J.13.

Private 11352 Ivan Stanley EADES 1st Battalion Coldstream Guards

Killed in action on the 25th January 1915. Born Newton-St-Loe, Somerset. Enlisted Devizes. Resident Melksham. He has no known grave and is commemorated on the Le Touret Memorial Panels 2 and 3.

200665 Private William George EDWARDS, 1st/4th Battalion Duke of Edinburgh's Wiltshire Regiment.

Killed in action on the 10th May 1918 aged 36 years. Son of Herbert and Eliza Edwards, of Trowbridge; husband of Emma Louisa Robinson (formerly Edwards), of 5, Gas Works Rd., Trowbridge, Wilts. He was born in Melksham. He is buried in Ramleh War Cemetery Egypt N.21.

208176 Private Robert James ELLERY, 7th Battalion North Staffordshire Regiment

Died on 5th July 1919 aged 37. Son of Fredrick William Ellery, of Broughton Gifford, Melksham, Wilts. He has no known grave and is commemorated on the Baku Memorial in Azerbaijan.

G/36092 Private Reginald Bertram ELLIS, Royal Sussex Regiment

Died on 1st November 1918 aged 30 years. Son of Albert and Jane Ellis, of Seend, Melksham. He is buried in Seend Holy Cross Churchyard.

Ordinary Seaman William Lot ESCOTT, S.S. Eskmere, Mercantile Marine

Killed on the 13th October 1917 aged 17 years old. Son of Alfred and Louise Jane Escott, of Atworth, Melksham, Wilts. He is commemorated on the Commonwealth War Dead Memorial: Tower Hill Memorial. The SS Eskmere was a defensively armed British Merchant steamer. On the 13th October 1917 when on route from Belfast for Barry she was torpedoed by German submarine UC-75 and sunk when 15 miles WNW from South Stack, Anglesey, Wales. 20 lives were lost including the ships Master

8772 Private George William FARMER, 3rd Battalion Bedfordshire Regiment & Labour Corps.

Died 20th July 1918 aged 39 years. Son of Joseph and Mary Farmer, of Ampthill; husband of Rose Elizabeth Farmer, of Corsham Rd. Whitley, Melksham, Wilts. He is buried in Ampthill St Andrew Churchyard ref I.Z.4.

Picture courtesy Mr Ian Church

 ### K/28 Leading Stoker Charles Edward FULLER, H.M.S Queen Mary, Royal Navy

Killed in action on the 31st May 1916 at the Battle of Jutland. Son of James and S. A. Fuller, of Drynham, Trowbridge, Wilts. Native of Broughton Gifford, Melksham, Wilts. He is commemorated on the Portsmouth Naval Memorial ref 16.

"Charles Edward Fuller was 26 years of age, was the eldest son of Mr James Fuller of Challymead, Broughton Gifford. He held the position of Leading Stoker on HMS Queen Mary, and had been in the Navy for about eight years. Prior to that he worked for Mr Gore at the mattress factory at Broughton Gifford, and as a boy attended the Broughton Gifford School. He was also connected with

*the Wesleyan Sunday School and for some years rendered useful help. He was
well known and much respected in the village and its locality and much sympathy
is felt for his parent and the family in their bereavement."*
(Picture and text courtesy Wiltshire Times)

Forward guns of HMS Queen Mary

CHARLES EDWARD FULLER.

3/395 Lance Corporal Walter Charles Frank GAY, 1st Battalion Duke of Edinburgh's Wiltshire Regiment

Killed in action on the 25th September 1915 aged 18 years
old. He was born in Bradford on Avon he enlisted in
Trowbridge and at that time was resident in Melksham.
Son of Harry and Hester Gay, of The Common, Broughton
Gifford, Melksham, Wilts. He has no known grave and is
commemorated on Panel 53 on the Ypres Menin Gate
memorial.

*"Lance Corporal Gay was aged 18 years and was a
valued employee at the Avon Rubber Works at Melksham.
With the outbreak of war and the clarion cry "To Arms"
young Gay, without hesitation threw up his job and joined the forces of the King.
He was attached to the 3rd Wilts Regiment and was sent to Weymouth were his
preliminary training was undergone. His aptitude for gunnery was early
recognized and he was appointed to the machine gun section. Early in June he
arrived in France and was then attached to the 1st Battalion with whom he had
since seen much active service. The first news of his death was contained in a
letter from Pte G Hornblow of Melksham, who intimated in a letter to a friend that
"young Gay died a soldier's death." A further letter was received from Captain
Hales of the 1st Wilts who, writing to Mrs Gay says: "It is with the greatest regret
that I have to inform you of your son's death during the heavy bombardment of
September 25th. He died instantaneously and without pain. He had just got his*

Lance Corporal stripe and had he been spared would have received further promotion.

Lance Corporal Gay was a keen advocate of sport and was constantly seen in the ranks of Broughton United Football Club. He was also a member of the Parish Church choir and Sunday school, and on Sunday evening the Rev Rowland Davis in the course of his sermon alluded to the sad event and said the prayers and sympathy of the congregation would go out to the bereaved parents.

Pte Harry Gay father of the deceased soldier is a member of the National Reserve now on duty in Birmingham while another son, Trooper Herbert Gay is with the Royal Wiltshire yeomanry at Canterbury. Three other members of Mr Gay's family are with the colours, two being in the National Reserve and one with the 2nd Wilts in France."

(Picture and text courtesy Wiltshire Times)

Extract of Battalion War Diary Saturday 25th September 1915

Report covering these operations.

Positions were taken up on the night of 24th/25th as follows:-

B Coy new slits SE of old assembly trenches S of MENIN road. A Coy 2 platoons H12. 2 platoons new trench dug 60 yds to rear of H12. D Coy RS5. C Coy 2 platoons RS4 2 platoons HALF WAY HOUSE C&D Coys were carrying until 1.30a.m. Battn was in position by 2a.m. Battn dressing station and HQ

were completed close to RS5. The bombardment commenced at 3.50a.m. and the enemy bombardment commenced at 3.50a.m. and the enemy replied within 30

seconds by fierce artillery fire on front line and CTs, chiefly with field guns and small How's. A curtain of shrapnel was put in front of H12 and the assembly trenches there which was maintained for 2 hours. The MENIN Rd was swept with shrapnel as were the main CTs, GRAFTON, UNION & CASTLE Streets.

HE shrapnel was put over H12 (A Coy) and the slits S of MENEN Road (B Coy). Telephone wires to all trenches & Bde HQ were immediately cut. The trenches occupied by Battn did not suffer much from heavy shell fire except the left of RS5 (D Coy) which was badly blown in at junctions of CTs. Certain other points were obviously marked and a constant fire of shrapnel was kept up at these places throughout the day. The main CTs were blown in, in many places but were not rendered unserviceable. During the operations they were of the utmost value for evacuating the wounded & relieving congestion in the front lines.

A t 7.30a.m. in an order to move up 1 Coy to the firing line was received from Bde HQ. This was carried out by B Coy who occupied a portion of C6, C7 having A Coy RIR on their left and a small party of 2nd S Lancs on the right. Later in the day the front line was considered to be too crowded and 1 platoon of this Coy was withdrawn to CTs. N of MENIN Road 3 M Guns of the Battn were in position in the firing line to support the attack & 1 in reserve. The two right hand guns were put out of action and the emplacements destroyed by shell fire. The disposition of the Battn after B Coy had moved up remained unchanged during the day.

Heavy shelling continued during the day C6 C5 suffered severely also CTs from Crater to fire trenches, there were bombed in places and very little cover against shrapnel remained in the right sector.

No definite information was received as to the result of the attack. It was believed that 2 Coys of the RIR had gone forward. In our original fire trenches now occupied by B Coy, Wilts, A Coy RIR and details of other regiments nothing was known as to the position in front and no communication was established with the Coys who had gone forward. The situation was very uncertain. Our troops on the left were observed to retire from the enemies trenches which had apparently been captured, it was reported by a Sgt that they lost heavily by M gun enfilade fire in doing so.

Orders were received at 7.30p.m. for the Battn to relieve the RIR & 2 S Lancs who had come back

to their original line.
Two Coys of the Battn were eventually moved up into the firing line with 2 M guns of the 4th S
Lancs to replace those put out of action. B Coy was relieved and sent back to dugouts at HALF
WAY HOUSE. D & C Coys garrisoned the firing line with A in the Support.
Relief of RIR and 2nd S Lancs was completed at about 1.30a.m. The enemy continued to shell the
CTs and approaches to front at intervals until 2a.m. The fire trenches especially on the right were
found to be in a very demolished condition and the line in front practically destroyed and many
dead were lying
about, a large number of bombs were buried and others rendered unserviceable.
The Battn at the end of the day consisted of 400 rifles the majority of whom were in a very
exhausted condition. There had been very few opportunities of
getting any sleep during the past week.

6113 Private Edgar William GODWIN 10th Battalion King's (Liverpool Regiment)

Died at home on the 3rd February 1917. Enlisted in Bradford on Avon and was living in Atworth, Melksham at the time of his call up. Formerly 26180 in the Wiltshire Regiment. He is buried in Seagry (St Mary) Churchyard Near North-West corner of Church.

J/1655 Alfred John GOSS, H.M.S. Monmouth Royal Navy

Killed in action on the 1st November 1914 aged 23 years old. Son of Thomas W. and Emma Goss, of Church St, Atworth, Melksham, Wilts. He is commemorated on the Plymouth Naval Memorial Ref 1.

On the outbreak of the Great War HMS Monmouth was reactivated from the reserve and sent to join the 4th Cruiser Squadron (the West Indies Squadron) of Admiral Sir Christopher Cradock. She participated in the Battle of Coronel off the coast of Chile on1st November 1914. Outmatched and with an inexperienced crew, she was quickly overwhelmed, being unable to use many of her guns due to

the stormy weather. Early in the battle, a 21 cm (8.2 inch) shell from the Gneisenau penetrated the armour of the forward 6 inch gun turret, destroying it and causing a massive fire on the forecastle. More serious hits followed, and she soon could no longer hold her place in the line of battle. When it was clear that *Monmouth* was out of action, Gneisenau shifted its attention to HMS Good Hope. A short while later, drifting and on fire, Monmouth was attacked by the newly arrived light cruiser Nurnberg

which fired seventy-five 10.5 cm (4.1 inch) shells at close range. Monmouth and Good Hope both sank with a combined loss of 1,570 lives. There were no survivors from either ship.

 J/13016 Able Seaman Hedley Alexander GRANT, H.M Submarine 'L10' Royal Navy

Killed in action on the 4th October 1918 aged 23 years old. Son of William and May Grant, of "Roselea" Ringwood Rd, Parkstone, Dorset. He was born in Melksham, Wilts. He has no known grave and is commemorated on the Portsmouth Naval Memorial ref 29.

 Private 18067 John GREGORY Machine Gun Corps

Killed in action on the 20th May 1916. He was born in Melksham, enlisted in Devizes. Formerly 7505 Wiltshire Regiment. He is buried in Ecoivers Military Cemetery Mon-St Eloi grave II.C.25.

7007 Private James GREGORY, 1ˢᵗ Battalion Duke of Edinburgh's Wiltshire Regiment

Killed in action on the 20ᵗʰ June 1917. He was born in Melksham and prior to enlisting in Salisbury he was residing in Chippenham. He has no known grave and is commemorated on the Ypres Menin Gate Memorial Panel 53.

 ### 13859 Private Frederick GUNSTONE, 10ᵗʰ Battalion Devonshire Regiment

Killed in action on the 1ˢᵗ May 1917 aged 22 years. Younger son of Frank and Elizabeth Gunstone, of 5, New Rd. Buildings, Twerton-on-Avon, Bath. He was born in Melksham and enlisted in Bath. He is buried in the Sarigol Military Cemetery, Kriston, Greece.

From April to June 1917, the 35th Casualty Clearing Station was at Sarigol. It was replaced by the 21st Stationary Hospital, which remained until December 1918. From these two hospitals, 150 burials were made in the cemetery, many of them men who had been wounded in the Allied attack on the Grand-Couronne and Pip Ridge in April-May 1917.

 ### 22471 Private William Henry GUNSTONE 2ⁿᵈ Battalion Duke of Edinburgh's Wiltshire Regiment.

Killed in action on the 19ᵗʰ October 1918 aged 36. He was born in Melksham son of Henry and Ellen Miriam Gunstone, of Priory St., Corsham, Wilts; husband of Ada F. R. Gunstone, of Priory St., Corsham, Wilts. He is buried in St Aubert British Cemetery IC.D.

 ### S/16036 Rifleman Arthur Robert William HALL, 12ᵗʰ Battalion Rifle Brigade

Killed in action on the 18ᵗʰ August 1917 aged 20 years. He was born in Melksham and was the son of Arthur James and Rosina Hall, of 127, Queen's Rd., Peckham, London. He has no known grave and is commemorated on the Tyne Cot Memorial Panel 145 to 147.

9549 Private Edward George Hancock, 1st Battalion Somerset Light Infantry

Killed in action on the 25th May 1915 aged 22 years. He was born at Norrington Common Melksham and was son of George Hancock, of Moor Green, Corsham, Wilts. He has no known grave and is commemorated on the Ypres Menin Gate Memorial panel 21.

35178 Private George Frederick HARDING, 6th Battalion Duke of Edinburgh's Wiltshire Regiment

Killed in action on the 10th April 1918 aged 19 years. Son of George Fredrick and Annie Harding, of The Common, Broughton Gifford, Melksham, Wilts. He has no known grave and is commemorated on the Tyne Cot memorial panels 119 to 120.

Extract from Battalion War Diary H.Q. 58th Inf. Bde April 1918

Herewith Narrative of Events from 10th April - 20th April during operations

near WYTSCHAETE. 6th Wiltshire Yeomanry Battn. The Wiltshire Regt.

On the night of the 9/10th April the Battn. was holding a sub sector of the trenches east of the MESSINES - WYTSCHAETE ridge - with its right on the WAMBEKE & its left on JUNCTION BUILDINGS (exclusive). The front was held by two Coys. (A & B) which were distributed in depth - each with two platoons in the front line of posts & 1 strong platoon in support. C & D Coys. Were in reserve about 2000 yds. Behind the front line.
About 3.30a.m. fairly heavy shelling on the whole sub sector began consisting of H.E. & gas shells. This continued practically without intermission the whole day though no gas shells fell after about 5.30a.m.
About 6.a.m. the shelling which was much heavier on the sub sector of the Battalion on our right reached a climax, and the enemy under cover of a very thick "scotch mist" attacked the 57th Bde. On the right & apparently forced its centre Battn. back on to its reserve line. The left Battalion of the 57th Bde (the 10th Warwick R.) thereby had its right flank turned & the success of the attack was so sudden that a portion of the Warwick's were forced to fall back in a northerly direction on to our right flank - the WAMBEKE formed the natural boundary between the 57th & 58th Bdes. - & just North of it ran a long duck-boarded but shallow Communication trench. MANCHESTER ST. between VERNE RD. & GUN farm was a system of flooded shallow trenches, which "C" Coy. Occupied at once to form a defensive position, while half the support platoon of B Coy. was utilized with any parties of the 10th WARWICK R. which came across the BEKE to man MANCHESTER ST. as a long defensive flank.
The 4th Coy. (D Coy) was used to stiffen up the defence of the right flank of the Bde which was so dangerously exposed.
The whole Battalion Sub sector was subjected to heavy shelling and a large part of it to M.G. & rifle fire throughout the day, the M.G. & rifle fire coming from the high ground South of WAMBEKE round ANZAC FARM.
The Bn. maintained its position everywhere until 4.30p.m. that afternoon. At 3.30p.m. the enemy was massing 2000 yds. east of our front line - & a frontal attack developed, but was unable to

materialise owing to our vigorous Lewis & gun rifle fire.

At 4.30p.m. orders were received by the Battn. on our left (9th R.W.F.) to evacuate the front line of posts; & as this order emanated from Bde. the front line held by this Bn. was also abandoned, although the order for this to be done never reached the front line from our Bn. H.Q. A strong position was then taken up by the two front Coys on a line of supporting points. The enemy advanced about 5.30p.m. to our original front line, but was unable to approach nearer than 600 or 800 yds. owing to our active Lewis gun & rifle fire.

About 6p.m. the enemy organised strong attacks on our right & left flanks - The order to withdraw on to the Reserve Line never reached the front line Coys. so our position on the support line were held until the enemy had completely

surrounded the two front line Coy. A few elements of which, only, managed to work through to our own lines.

The reserve Coys. Which had been heavily engaged on the right flank, fell back fighting on to the high ground WEST of COSTAVERNE. Battn. H.Q. Coy. Which

 was utilised in an attempt to strengthen the right rear was also engaged heavily in fighting in which the C.O. Major Monreal was mortally wounded & the 2nd in Command Capt. Garthwaite wounded. During the night the survivors of the battn. rallied on portions of the front between the DAMMSTRASSE & WYTSCHAETE. 75 stragglers were collected & sent up to GRAND BOIS, where Capt. Rentoul had established Bn. H.Q. The remainder of the day was spent in collecting & re-organising the Battn.

Private 14288 Francis William HORNBLOW 6th Battalion Duke of Edinburgh's Wiltshire Regiment.

Killed in action on the 14th July 1917 aged 24 years. He enlisted in Trowbridge and resident in Melksham at the time of his call up. Son of Samuel and Emily Hornblow, of 12, Calstone, Calne, Wilts. Buried Oosttaverne Wood Cemetery III.A.13

200750 Lance Corporal Henry HILLIER, 1st/4th Battalion Duke of Edinburgh's Wiltshire Regiment

Killed in action on the 14th November 1917 aged 24 years. Son of Henry James and Henrietta Hillier, of Ivy Cottage, Seend, Melksham, Wilts. He is buried in Deir El Belah War Cemetery, Egypt, Ref B.81.

*7667/202992 Private Reginald Genvy KAYNES, 1st Battalion Middlesex Regiment or 1st Battalion Duke of Edinburgh's Wiltshire Regiment**

Killed in action on the 16th May 1917 aged 21 years. Son of William and the late Florence Edith Kaynes, foster son of Mary Anne Hemmings, of Box Cottage, Whitley, Melksham, Wilts. Born at Chippenham, Wilts. He is buried in Henin Communal Cemetery Extension ref II.B.7.

"Born Chippenham 5th September 1895 and educated at Shaw School, Melksham. He enlisted May 1916 and served with the Expeditionary force in France and Flanders from the following November. He died at the 55th Field Ambulance on 16th May 1917 of wounds he received in action near Monchy-le-Preux. He was buried there 2 miles behind the firing line. He was keenly interested in football. Following the official information of his death many letters were received from

officers and comrades which proved to Mrs Hemmings that he had inspired the same respect and esteem as he shared among his friends at home. Mrs Hemmings of Box Cottage, Whitley, near Melksham received official intimation on Wednesday last week that her adopted son Private Reginald Genvy Kaynes, Middlesex Regiment had been killed in action on May 16th. The news made the whole village a place of mourning for among the many who have left the place to serve King and country none was more generally liked that Reginald Kaynes. He was 21 years of age and had been in the Army since May 1915. As a boy he attended the Wesleyan Sunday School and the day school at Shaw, and was later keenly interested in the Football Club, playing in several matches.

Following the official intimation Mrs Hemmings received a letter from the Quarter Master Sergeant which showed among his comrades Private Kaynes had inspired the same respect and esteem as he shared among his neighbours at home. A brother of Pte Kaynes, Cecil, is in the Royal Marine Light Infantry. He was formerly on the "Black Prince) but left this ship to take on land service shortly before she was sunk in the battle off Jutland. He is now on sick leave, having lost an eye in the fighting in France. Much Sympathy is felt with Mrs Hemmings with whom the brothers have lived since their very early days. "
(Picture and text courtesy Wiltshire Times)

* R.G.Kaynes is listed on the CWGC website as serving with The Wiltshire Regiment yet his Medal Index Card at the National Archive and his obituary in de Ruvigney's both list him as serving in the Middlesex Regiment. The above picture and the article reproduced from The Wiltshire Times also list him as being a member of the Middlesex Regiment. On the Roll of Honour in the Whitley Reading Rooms he is listed as being in the Middlesex Regiment. At the time of going to print I am in correspondence with the Commonwealth War Graves Commission to have him properly recognised. Until such time as I can conclusively prove that his Regiment was the Middlesex I have listed him with both regimental badges.

132171 Private Rowland John KEEN, 19th Company Machine Gun Corps

Killed in action 10th April 1918 aged 19 years old. Son of Albert and Jane Keen, of Broughton Gifford, Melksham, Wilts. He has no known grave and is commemorated on Tyne Cot Memorial Panels 154 to 159 and 163A.

135429 Lance Bombardier Clifford Victor Skulthorpe LITTLE, 'D' Battery, 15th Brigade Royal Field Artillery

Killed in action on the 23rd August 1918. Son of Thomas Little, of Challymead House, Melksham. He is buried in Gommecourt British Cemetery No 2 Hebuterne. Ref V.G.17.

22323 Private Samuel LOVE, 2nd Battalion Duke of Edinburgh's Wiltshire Regiment

Killed in action on the 26th April 1918 aged 39 years old. Son of William and Mary Love, of King St, Melksham, Wilts. husband of Rhoda Love, of 21, Tory Rank, Bradford-on-Avon. He has no known grave and is commemorated on Tyne Cot Memorial Panels 119 to 120.

7601 Private William George MACE, 'C' Company 1st Battalion Duke of Edinburgh's Wiltshire Regiment

Killed in action on the 2nd November 1914 aged 25 years. Son of William and Hannah Mace, of Minister House, Folley Lane, Shaw, Melksham, Wilts. He has no known grave and is commemorated on Ploegsteert Memorial Panel 8.

Extract from Battalion War Diary Monday 2nd November 1914

Strength return through draft received yesterday brings us up to 13 officers 521 other ranks. Day spent in cleaning up and getting rifles etc in working condition.
2p.m. received an order to stand by "ready to go to the assistance of the French troops about WYTSTCHAETE" E of here. We were not sent out, ordered to close up in billets to make room for French troops.

Captain Arthur Curgenven MAGOR, 3rd Battalion Duke of Edinburgh's Wiltshire Regiment, Attached 2nd Battalion

Killed in Action on 17th October 1914. He has no known grave and he is commemorated on the Ypres Menin Gate Memorial Panel 53.

Extract from war diary Saturday 17th October 1914.

Firing line opened fire about 1am nothing of the enemy was seen although a few shots were returned presumably from a patrol. Capt Magor was killed. Battalion remained in trenches all day.

Probationer Nurse Grace Margaret MARLEY, Territorial Force Nursing Service

Daughter of Mrs. Catherine S. Marley of The Briars, 11, Sandridge Rd., Melksham. She was based at 2nd Southern General Hospital. She died at Bristol following a very serious operation on 12th October 1916. The memorial service took place at the chapel of the Royal Infirmary attended by the matron (Miss Baillie), sisters and domestic staff. At Melksham, the first part of the service was held in the parish church and in addition to relatives, present were Colonel Prowse (2nd Southern General Hospital), Sister Kennedy and Nurses Smith, Hardiman and Withershaw of the Royal Infirmary, Bristol. The grave memorial is a recumbent granite cross 4'6" high with inscribed matching kerbs and chippings. The cross bears the inscription "Thy will be done" whilst the kerbing has the inscription "Ever loving memory of Grace Margaret, daughter of Duncan and Catherine Marley. Died October 12th 1916 aged 23 years. Her name, as a Special Military Probationer, was on a marble tablet in the chapel of
Queen Alexandra's Military Hospital, Millbank, London which lists the names of the matrons, sisters and nurses of the military nursing services who died during WW1. The Millbank site was redeveloped and the memorial has been traced to the Royal Garrison Church, Farnborough Road, Aldershot, Hampshire.
(My thanks to Mr Jim Strawbridge for the above information

Grace Margaret Marley's grave in Melksham Churchyard

2194 Private William Alfred MATTOCK, 9th Battalion Royal Irish Fusiliers

Killed in action on the 11th October 1918 aged 34 years old. Son of Alfred Mattock, of 6, Innox Rd., Trowbridge, Wilts; husband of Nellie Mattock, of Seend View, Seend, Melksham, Wilts. He has no known grave and is commemorated on the Tyne Cot Memorial Panels 140 to 141.

Herbert John MERCHANT Private 260472 12th Battalion Gloucestershire Regiment

Died of Wounds received in action on the 5th December 1918. Originally enlisted in Newport as 315411 Pte in the Monmouthshire Regiment. Buried Seend Cleeve Chapel Cemetery (Front row of right plot)

8727 Corporal W.F. MERRETT, Duke of Edinburgh's Wiltshire Regiment

8727 Corporal Wiltshire Regiment. Son of Mrs M.A. Merrett, 26 Scotland Road, Melksham. Died 25th March 1920 aged 31. Buried Beanacre (St Barnabas) Churchyard.

 142995 Private Francis Richard MOBEY, 25th Battalion Machine Gun Corps

Killed in action on the 10th April 1918 aged 32 years old. Son of the late William and Ellen Mobey; husband of Emily Maria Mobey, of 33, Woodrow Rd, Melksham, Wilts. He has no known grave and is commemorated on the Terlinchthun Memorial Panel 11.

33047 Private Ralph NEWMAN, 1st Battalion Duke of Edinburgh's Wiltshire Regiment

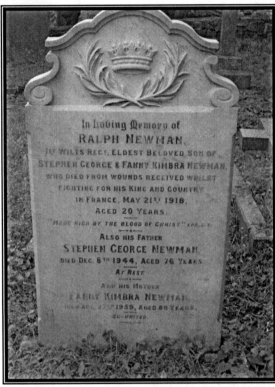

Died on 21st May 1918 aged 20 years old from wounds. Son of Stephen George and Fanny Kimbra Newman, of Rew Farm, Seend, Melksham. He is buried in Seend Holy Cross Churchyard

33250 Private William NICHOLSON, 2nd Battalion Duke of Edinburgh's Wiltshire Regiment

Killed in Action on the 31st July 1917. Born Barton St David, he enlisted in Trowbridge and was resident in Melksham at the time of his call up. He has no known grave and is commemorated on the Ypres Menin Gate Memorial Panel 53.

Sapper 267994 Frederick Guy NORRIS 18th Division Signal Company Royal Engineers

Died on the 6th July 1919 aged 34. Son of Frederick and Emma Norris, of Trowbridge, Wilts. He was resident in Melksham at the time of his call up. Buried Terlinchthun British Cemetery Wimille, France.

201535 Lance Corporal William Frederick OSBORN, 1st/4th Battalion Duke of Edinburgh's Wiltshire Regiment.

Died on the 18th September 1917 aged 25 years. He was born in Melksham and enlisted in Trowbridge but prior to the war he is listed as living with his mother, Charlotte Osborn, of 17, Queen St., Upper Weedon, Northants, and the late Samuel Osborn. He is buried in Cape Town, Maitland Cemetery Sec.4.97194C.

SS/23202 Private J.A. OWEN Royal Army Service Corps

Son of George and Elizabeth Owen of St Michaels Bristol. Husband of Rosa Emma Shelland (Formerly Owen) of 211, Coronation Road, Southville, Bristol. Died 6th November 1919 Aged 48 Years. Buried Melksham Church Cemetery.

128402 Gunner Herbert PARFITT, 'D' Battery 157th Brigade Royal Field Artillery

Died of Wounds on 24th August 1918 aged 24. Son of Margaret Parfitt, of Morgan's Cottage, Bowerhill, Melksham, Wilts., and the late William Parfitt. Native of Seend, Melksham. He is buried in Arneke British Cemetery ref III. E. 18.

112 Corporal C. PARK, 5th Battalion Duke of Edinburgh's Wiltshire Regiment

Died on the 9th September 1919 aged 34. Son of Mrs. Louisa Park, of 19, Woodrow Rd, The Forest, Melksham. He is buried at South end of new part Melksham Church Cemetery

18565 Private Arthur Leslie PARSONS, 3rd Battalion South Wales Borderers

Died at home on the 12th October 1918. He was born in Melksham and is shown as having enlisted in Newport, South Wales near to where he was living in Blackwood Monmouthshire at the time. He is buried in Bedwellty, St Sannan Churchyard 2.3.26.

51303 Private Percy Reginald RANDALL, 10th Battalion Worcestershire Regiment

Killed in action on the 24th April 1918. Percy was born in Melksham and at the time of his enlistment he is listed as living in Trowbridge. He is buried in the La Clytte Military Cemetery V.D.21.

18136 Private Arthur ROGERS, 2nd Battalion Duke of Edinburgh's Wiltshire Regiment

Killed in Action on the 15th June 1915 aged 21 years old. Son of Herbert and Elizabeth Rogers, of Beanacre, Melksham, Wilts. He enlisted in Devizes. He has no known grave and is commemorated on the Le Touret Memorial Panel 33 and 34.

Extract from Battalion War Diary

During the day trench J7 - 15 was shelled and the defenders (2 platoons of each 'C' & 'D' Coys) suffered a few casualties. At 6pm the battalion commenced to attack the line 112, J14 -J13. On quitting their trenches, the leading companies ('C' & 'D') were subjected to a heavy frontal and enfilade fire, the latter from 14 - 19. As the advance progressed it was enfiladed by machine gun fire from both flanks, on the right from the foot of the hill between 112 & 13, on the left from machine guns concealed in the grass somewhere west of J13 'B' coy followed in support of 'C' & 'D' and occupied J9 -15. 'A' coy in reserve in Scottish trench. 'A' Company had been kept in reserve intact, as it had orders to make a reconnaissance after the position had been captured, the reconnaissance to be on VIOLAINES. The firing line reached a point about 50 yards west of German
trench at J14. There was then only one officer not hit in the two leading companies.
At 7.5pm half 'A' company went forward to endeavour to push on the attack which had been held up. This half company with half 'D' company then advanced, and were subjected to enfilade fire from the crater, and could not advance beyond the disused Old German trench.
At 9pm the situation was as follows:-
The regiment was occupying the old German trench, with 'C' & 'D' Coys in front of them, and the trench J7 - 15, and were in touch with the Grenadier Guards on left of J7. Groups from 'C' & 'D' companies were returning to old German trench from the front. Orders were received to attack the German line at 9.15pm in conjunction with the Bedford Regt & Yorkshire Regt. The time was subsequently altered to 10pm. In order to form up for the attack the companies which were holding the old German trench & were being enfiladed from the right were ordered back to Scottish trench with orders to form up in rear of it to clear the field of fire of the company holding J7 - 15. The order to attack was subsequently cancelled as far as the Regiment was concerned, and instructions were received to hand over the trenches to the Bedford Regt and return to WINDY CORNER. During the action of 15th 16th, the Germans used incendiary bullets, and also sniped the wounded in front of their trenches.

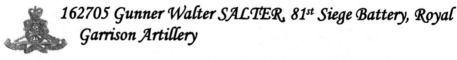 *162705 Gunner Walter SALTER, 81st Siege Battery, Royal Garrison Artillery*

Killed in action on the 17th October 1918. Walter was born in Seend, Melksham and at the time of his enlistment into the Artillery he was living and working in Melksham. He is buried in the Niagra Cemetery, Iwuy, France, E.1.

34390 Lance Corporal Henry SARTAIN, 8th Battalion York and Lancaster Regiment.

Henry was killed in action on the 28th April 1917 aged 24 years. He was born in Melksham and is shown as having initially joined the Hussars as 18094 Private Sartain. He enlisted in Basingstoke and was son of Henry and Clara Eleanor Sartain, of Waits Farm, Headley, Newbury, Berks. He is buried in the Lijssenthoek Military Cemetery XII.A.24A.

 ### *806 Pte Harry SEWARD 2nd Battalion Rhodesia Regiment 1st East African Brigade.*

Killed in action on the 11th March 1916 aged 33. Son of George Underhill Seward and Elizabeth Seward, of Seend, Melksham, Wilts. Born at Bridgwater, Somerset. He is buried in Taveta Military Cemetery Kenya ref IX. A. 6.

Private Seward was killed during the fighting at Latema-Reata Nek, after the Germans had withdrawn to formidable positions in the Kitovo Hills, which were densely wooded and easily capable of defence. On the morning of the 11th March the British made a general advance under the command of General Malleson, a mixed force consisting of the 3rd King's African Rifles, the 130th Baluchis, the 2nd Rhodesians, Belfield's Scouts, the Mounted Infantry Company, and field and howitzer batteries, besides machine-guns, including those of the Loyal North Lancashires. About noon General Malleson advanced to attack the spur of Latema, which commanded the nek from the north, but made little headway. The enemy had plenty of cover, and from the bush-clad slopes of the hill maintained so severe a gun and rifle fire that the British were held up. Casualties suffered by the Rhodesians on 11th March were:- killed 15, missing 2, severely wounded 11, wounded 23 & slightly wounded 9. This was out of a force of 16 officers and 525 rank and file.

(Picture courtesy Mr Harry Fecitt.)

 J/53836 Ordinary Seaman William Charles SHADWELL, H.M.S. Paragon Royal Navy

Killed in action on the 17th March 1917 aged 32 years old. Son of James and Susan Shadwell, of Melksham, Wilts; husband of Elizabeth Mary Shadwell, of 18, Station Rd, Ashford, Kent. He is commemorated on the Portsmouth Naval Memorial.

 The destroyer HMS *Paragon,* was patrolling the submarine barrage in the Straits of Dover on the night of March 17th, 1917, in company with the *Laertes, Laforey* and *Llewellyn.* At about 10.50 p.m. a German destroyer force led by Cdr. Tillessen steamed into the Straits with the object of breaking the barrage. The first ship to encounter them was the *Paragon,* which was torpedoed and overwhelmed with gunfire when in the act of flashing her challenge. She was hit by a torpedo and gunfire and broke in half within eight minutes and sank. Some of her own depth charges exploded killing some of the survivors; only ten of her complement of 77 being picked up. The *Llewellyn,* which came on the scene in time to rescue the few survivors, was also torpedoed but, fortunately, did not sink.

 Second Lieutenant Sydney Bicheno SMITH, Royal Garrison Artillery.

Died on the 1st December 1918 aged 35 years, husband of Dorothy May Kennedy Smith of 18 Hedge Lane, Palmers Green, London. Buried in Camberwell Old Cemetery Grave reference 85.25569.

"The death is also announced as the result of wounds received in action of the Rev S.B. Smith, B.D, Second Lieutenant, R.A., fourth son of the Rev W and Mrs Smith of Melksham, who succumbed on Sunday at the 4th General Military Hospital, London. The deceased, who was well known in Melksham, had been serving in France. "(Text courtesy of Wiltshire Times)

8229 *Private Alfred John SMITH, 1ˢᵗ Battalion Duke of Edinburgh's Wiltshire Regiment*

Killed in action on the 3ʳᵈ September 1916 aged 28 years old. Son of John Smith; husband of Evelyn May Smith, of 1, Burnt Cottage, Beanacre, Melksham, Wilts. He has no known grave and is commemorated on the Theipval memorial Pier and Face 13A.

Extract from Battalion War Diary

In the trenches. Orders had been received previously that the Battn would take the trenches R31.C.78, R31.A.48, R.31.a5.5, R.31.a.9.41, R.31.a9.3, R.31.b.0.3, 2.3,3.2,3.1,5.1,5.0, R31.d.7..9,9.8. Late on the night of the 2nd/3rd written orders were received that the only attack to be made were upon the lines, R.31.C.4.6 to R.31.a.5.5 and upon R.31.c.7.6 to R.31.a.9.1, R.31.d.4.8., R.31.d.07. This meant that both the flanks of this Battn were exposed. The Battn arrived in position in trenches at 2.30 without casualty in spite of heavy shelling. The intense bombardment began at 5.10a.m. and the troops moved out of the trenches and formed up about 50 yards off and advanced upon their objective. As soon as they had left the trench they were met by a heavy 'whiz-bang' fire, and almost at the same time machine guns from either flank opened upon them. Our right Coy (D) stated that they got into the enemy trench and were wiped out by our own barrage which did not lift in time. The centre and
left Coys report that their heavy losses were due to machine gun fire from both flanks. By the time they reached their objective they were numerically inferior to the enemy. The left Coy reached and occupied R.31.C.8.9. And made a block there. The few men in the other Coys who reached the enemy trench were forced to retire owing to their lack of numbers. The true position was not known at this time, and the reserve Coy was sent up to strengthen the line, but as far as could be ascertained, they were knocked out by machine gun fire from the flanks. Shortly after the officers commanding right and centre Coys reported that they had been able to get back with infinite difficulty, and very few men and
that the attack had failed. The CO was hit by a bullet in the leg. Five other officers became casualties.
At about 11a.m. orders were received that the Battn should proceed back in small parties to BOUZINCOURT, which was duly undertaken. The last of the Battn arrived at their billets at about 5p.m.

 ## 53732 *Private Harry SMITH, 47ᵗʰ Battalion, Machine Gun Corps*

Killed in action on the 23ʳᵈ August 1918, He was born in Melksham and was working in Trowbridge prior to enlisting in Devizes. He is buried in Dernancourt Communal Cemetery Extension VII.A.29

20713 *Private Bertie SPARKS, Army Cyclist Corps*

Died on the 2nd November 1918 aged 19. Joined the Army Cyclist Corps before transferring to 437th Agricultural Company with service number 437834. Son of Alfred Sparks of Whitley. Buried at Shaw (Christ Church) Churchyard, Melksham Without.

18443 *Private William Herbert SPENCER, 2nd Battalion Duke of Edinburgh's Wiltshire Regiment*

Killed in action on the 15th June 1915 aged 19 years old. Son of Herbert and Edith Spencer, of Church Brook Cottage, Broughton Gifford, Melksham, Wilts. He has no known grave and is commemorated on the Le Touret Memorial Panel 33 and 34.

Extract from Battalion War Diary

During the day trench J7 - I5 was shelled and the defenders (2 platoons of each 'C' & 'D' Coys) suffered a few casualties. At 6pm the battalion commenced to attack the line I12, J14 -J13. On quitting their trenches, the leading companies ('C' & 'D') were subjected to a heavy frontal and enfilade fire, the latter from I4 - I9. As the advance progressed it was enfiladed by machine gun fire from both flanks, on the right from the foot of the hill between I12 & I3, on the left from machine guns concealed in the grass somewhere west of J13 'B' coy followed in support of 'C' & 'D' and occupied J9 -I5. 'A' coy in reserve in Scottish trench. 'A' Company had been kept in reserve intact, as it had orders to make a reconnaissance after the position had been captured, the reconnaissance to be on VIOLAINES. The firing line reached a point about 50 yards west of German trench at J14. There was then only one officer not hit in the two leading companies. At 7.5pm half 'A' company went forward to endeavour to push on the attack which had been held up. This half company with half 'D' company then advanced, and were subjected to enfilade fire from the crater, and could not advance beyond the disused Old German trench. At 9pm the situation was as follows:-
The regiment was occupying the old German trench, with 'C' & 'D' Coys in front of them, and the trench J7 - I5, and were in touch with the Grenadier Guards on left of J7. Groups from 'C' & 'D' companies were returning to old German trench from the front. Orders were received to attack the German line at 9.15pm in conjunction with the Bedford Regt & Yorkshire Regt. The time was

subsequently altered to 10pm. In order to form up for the attack the companies which were holding the old German trench & were being enfiladed from the right were ordered back to Scottish trench with orders to form up in rear of it to clear the field of fire of the company holding J7 - 15. The order to attack was subsequently cancelled as far as the Regiment was concerned, and instructions were received to hand over the trenches to the Bedford Regt and return to WINDY CORNER.

46753 Private Edward Forster TAYLOR, 'Z' Company 17th Battalion Lancashire Fusiliers

Killed in action on the 18th July 1918 aged 23 years. Son of Ernest Forster Taylor and Berthe Adele Taylor, of The Lodge, Shaw Hill, Melksham, Wiltshire. He is buried at Locre Hospice Cemetery ref Sp. Mem. A. 8.

5232 Private Albert TRIMNELL, 1st Battalion Duke of Edinburgh's Wiltshire Regiment

Killed in action on the 26th October 1914. Born Poulshot Enlisted Devizes resident Melksham Killed in Action F&F 26th October 1914

Extract from the Battalion War Diary for the date Monday 26 Oct 1914 Neuve Chapelle

(Monday) Moved HQ back to farm. B & D Coys and two platoons A Coy in trenches. 2 platoons A Coy in support C Coy 80 strong, in reserve. About 1p.m. Enemy again shelled the trenches and vicinity of HQ very heavily. Regt on our left mostly cleared out of their trenches.
4.30p.m. heard enemy had come through on left of our trenches. Sent up 2 platoons in support, moved up reserve Coy closer just in time to meet the Germans debouching from W side of village of NEUVE CHAPELLE. Deployed 2 platoons of C Coy who held them at the HQ farm. Enemy came on to within 200 yards on the road, as it was getting dark, and they proceeded to entrench there. Deployed 3 platoons of C Coy and attacked them with the bayonet, drove them back into the burning village behind, killing and wounding a certain number of them and taking about 6 prisoners. Time about 6p.m. We are now informed that 2 Coys S Lancs, 2 Coys RIR and 2 Coys RF are coming to reinforce us. Arrange for a line to be made, and a general advance to be made to clear the village with the bayonet. Meanwhile, C Coy pushed up to the edge of the village. Great delay in getting the line forward. 5 different units, no senior officers to take command, no co-ordination. After waiting nearly an hour for a Regt on our left to come up the units of 7th Bde, Wilts, S Lancs, RIR (5 Coys in all), decided not to wait but push on to the relief of their comrades in the trenches. C Coy Wilts Regt formed the advance guard of the little force, and was led forward by Capt and Adj P S Rowan. We advanced to the S and middle of the village, and met with little opposition except from snipers. C Coy Wilts Regt pushed on down to left of our trenches and there found the adjoining trenches of the RIR which had been vacated and were now held by Germans. Capt Rowan led forward this party with gallantry, and, attacking the Germans with the bayonet, drove them back from RIR trenches, C Coy now occupied those trenches until the RIR come up. Rifles now put into these trenches and pushed up towards the left. Having seen this part of the task accomplished I, (Major Roche) returned to the village, where the other troops had waited. I there met with the other Commanding Officers and informed them that we were all right in our trenches, and Rifles rapidly getting theirs back, and urged that they should clear the rest of the town, and, re-establish the rest of the line on left of RIR held by the RF. The OC Royal Fusiliers who was the senior officer present, said that in approaching the W end of the village his

Battn came under heavy fire and suffered many casualties. After considerable delay and hesitation as to try and re-establish the firing in their trenches in front of the N end of the village of NEUVE CHAPELLE. It was eventually decided by the Senior Officer present that the N end of the village could not be attacked and cleared without Artillery support, and that to get this he must wait until daylight. All units about the village, which was now burning, withdrew to about half mile W of it, to about the line upon what the RF had been checked. I got the supplies up by hand, also ammunition, the road being rendered impossible by the holes from shell fire. These supplies and ammunition were got down to the trenches. I reinforced the trenches by 50 men of C Coy to replace casualties, and, withdrew about 3a.m. to my headquarters on W of village, having now with me only the HQ party of about 18 men and 40 men of C Coy under Capts Richards and Mee. During the night I discovered that a platoon of A Coy under 2nd Lieut Martin, who I thought had gone up to reinforce the trenches had not got there. I took half this platoon (1 & 12 men) and posted them about midway through the village with the object of preventing Germans in N end working down to S and again getting behind the trenches held by the Battn. The remainder of the platoon under 2nd Lieut Martin was directed to go back to the position it had been in, in support of the trenches.

Our casualties this day were: Capt M L Formby killed. Capt & Adj P S Rowan dangerously wounded, (Receiving two bullet wounds) this being the second time in this campaign this officer was wounded. Lieut Richardson severely wounded. 20 men killed, 40 men wounded, and 10 reported missing.

2899 Private Charles Havelock TYLER, 11th Australian Light Trench Mortar Battery

Died of Wounds 10th August 1918 aged 31 years. Son of William and Eliza Jane Tyler, of "The Garden," Shaw, Melksham, Wilts, England. Native of Erlestoke, nr. Devizes, England. He is buried in Brookwood Military Cemetery ref IV. I. 2.

Charles enlisted in Perth, Western Australia on the 29th September 1916 aged 29 years old. He was described as being about 5ft 9ins in height and having a fair complexion, blue eyes and brown hair. On the 16th October 1916 he was posted to the Depot to begin his basic training. On completion of training he was then posted to 44th Battalion and departed from Freemantle on the 29th December 1916 bound for England. He disembarked in Devonport from the Australian ship 'Persic' on the 3rd March 1917. After training at Larkhill Camp in Wiltshire his unit embarked for France on the 19th June 1917 where he was transferred to the 11th Light Trench Mortar Battery. He was slightly wounded on the 9th December 1917 and after some treatment at 9th Field Ambulance he was discharged back to duty. A Court of Inquiry was held to ascertain the reason for his wounds and the findings were recorded as…….*No 2899 Pte CH Tyler was Accidentally Wounded by a premature explosion of a Stokes Mortar Shell at PLOEGSTEERT on 9th Dec 1917.*

He continued to serve until 4th July 1918 when he was seriously wounded after being shot. He was taken to 4th Field Ambulance and then transferred to the 5th Casualty Clearing Station from where he was swiftly moved to Cambridge Hospital in Aldershot for specialist medical care. Unfortunately he succumbed to his wounds and died on 10th August 1918.

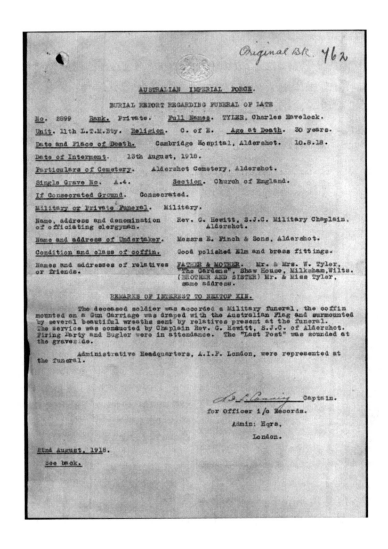

2495 Private Kenneth Leslie Bilbrough WALLIS, 1st/5th Battalion Northumberland Fusiliers

Son of John George Wallis, of "Tanglewood", 3 Forest Road, Melksham, Wiltshire. Born in Wallsend. He died on 30th December 1914 aged 22 years and is buried in Wallsend Church Bank Cemetery ref D. Gen274.

(Picture courtesy of Mr Andrew Round)

 ### *10956 Private Albert WAREHAM, 2nd Battalion Duke of Edinburgh's Wiltshire Regiment*

Killed in action on the 3rd December 1917 aged 31. Brother of Mabel Wareham of Manor Cottage, Seend, Melksham, Wiltshire. He is buried at Hooge Crater Cemetery ref XVII.J.16

Extract from Battalion War Diary

Our artillery very active at 5am. The 2nd New Zealand Infantry Brigade attacked POLDERHOEK CHATEAU zero 12noon. Enemy retaliated on our support and back areas B coy suffered 7 casualties.

30885 Private Charlie WEBB, 2nd Battalion Lancashire Fusiliers

He was killed in action on 6th September 1917 son of Joseph and Eliza Sarah Webb of Purlpit, Atworth, Melksham, Wiltshire. He was born in Bradford on Avon and enlisted in Trowbridge. He originally joined the Royal Engineers with service number 185808. He is buried in Happy Valley British Cemetery Fampoux ref C.2.

28050 Sergeant Harry WEBB, 2nd Battalion Hampshire Regiment

Killed in Action 30th September 1918 aged 23 years old. Son of Frederick and Mary Webb, of Melksham. Husband of Lilian Nellie Webb, of Broughton Gifford, Melksham, Wiltshire. Formerly 19033 8th Wiltshire Regiment. He is buried at Hooge Crater Cemetery Ref XVI.B.14

13913 Private Albert Ernest WHITE, 8th Battalion Norfolk Regiment

Killed in action on the 1st July 1916. Albert was born in Melksham and enlisted in Islington, Middlesex. He has no known grave and is commemorated on the Thiepval Memorial Pier and Face 1 C and 1 D.

3267 Corporal George WHITE, B Squadron 2nd Battalion Dragoon Guards (Queens Bays)

Killed in action 30th March 1918 aged 30 years. Son of the late Edmund and Frances White of Catford London, husband of Ellen White of 41, Dunch Rd, Melksham, Wiltshire. He is buried in St Pierre Cemetery, Amiens Ref IX.A.1.

2nd Lieutenant Thomas Geffrey WHITNEY, 3rd Battalion Royal Warwickshire Regiment

Son of Edward Whitney and Helen Amy Whitney, of Broad Oak, Groombridge, Sussex. Born at Nebea, New South Wales, Australia. Died 15th June 1916 aged 18 years old. Buried in Parkhurst Military Cemetery, Isle of Wight, Ref I.E.95.
(This is the only TG Whitney listed on the CWGC Website and apart from his entry on the Shaw & Whitley Roll of Honour and the Roll of Honour in Shaw Church I have been unable to establish his Melksham connection)

10966 Private Charles Frederick WILLIAMS, 1st Battalion Duke of Edinburgh's Wiltshire Regiment.

Killed in action on the 22nd June 1915 aged 17 years. Son of Frederick Charles and Mary Ann Williams, of 5, Market Place, Melksham, Wilts. He has no known grave and is commemorated on the Ypres Menin Gate Memorial Panel 53.

155572 Private Frederick YOUNG, 12th Machine Gun Corps

Killed in action on the 22nd September 1918 aged 18, son of Hubert and Edith Young of The Lodge, Broughton Gifford, Melksham, Wiltshire. He has no known grave and is commemorated on the Vis-en-Artois memorial Panel 10

12340 Guardsman William Henry YOUNG, 5th Battalion Grenadier Guards.

Died on the 30th November 1916 aged 39 years. He was born in Melksham and is shown as having enlisted in Cardiff. He died at home presumably from wounds and is buried in the Windsor Cemetery Berkshire R.25.

Throughout the war many families contributed to the war effort whether it was on the home front or in the armed forces. But there can be few who contributed as did the family Robinson from Melksham. The following appeared in the Wiltshire Times and is reproduced by kind permission.

A PATRIOTIC MELKSHAM FAMILY.

EIGHT SONS IN THE ARMY.

We have from time to time had the pleasure of recording some interesting items respecting Wiltshiremen who have done, and are doing, good service for their country in the present great war. In a number of instances several sons belonging to one family have been named, and their ready response to duty's call has reflected much credit on themselves and their relatives, as is the case with the family of Robinson, whose portraits are here produced. Eight sons serving with the Forces we believe constitutes a record for this part of the country, and a few details respecting the worthy father and his sons will be interesting.

The father, Mr. Elijah Robinson, now residing at the City, Melksham, has for some six years been a capable and valued worker of the Avon Indiarubber Company. Previously he was employed for some years at Calne. He is a true British soldier, having served upwards of twelve years in the 23rd Royal Fusiliers. He entered the Army in 1871, and took his discharge in 1883. His military career included a period of active service, as he went through the Ashantee War, in which he served under the late Sir Garnet Wolsley. He was fortunate enough to get through uninjured, and is the proud possessor of the war medal. Later, his regiment was called to take part in the Zulu campaign, but as it was on its way peace was declared, and arrangements were altered. Private Robinson then proceeded with his regiment to India, where he spent some years, with his family. Although now over 60 years of age he still has the military spirit in him, and is quite prepared to "do his bit" for the protection of his country. Since the war broke out he has on several occasions offered his services, and was much disappointed because his age prevented them being accepted. He is the proud father of twelve children, the eight sons here shown and four daughters.

Mrs. Robinson, who is a worthy helpmeet to her patriotic husband, has presented him with a family of 16, four of whom have died.

Our list gives the sons in the order of age, and it is gratifying to remark that although several of them have gone through some of the thickest fighting in France, neither has yet received a scratch. The eldest, however, Private James E. Robinson, of the Wilts, is now lying seriously ill in a military hospital at Birmingham. After serving in France he was transferred to Salonica, where he contracted dysentery and other complaints. He was treated for a time abroad, and afterwards brought back to England. He is a married man with three children. Prior to the war he was employed first at the Avon Rubber Works, then at the bacon factory at Chippenham, where his family are now residing. Like his father he showed the utmost readiness, when hostilities commenced, to fight for his country, and joined the Colours. The "slacker" community evidently does not meet with favour in the Robinson family.

Irad W. Robinson, now serving with the Grenadier Guards, acted on the same principle as his elder brother, and on the call of his country quitted his civil employment to join the Colours. Before the war he was managing a hotel in Gloucester.

William A. Robinson, who was in the service of a gentleman as chauffeur, at High Wycombe, is now in the A.S.C., M.T., France.

Wilfred George, the fourth son, is also in the A.S.C., at present in England. He was formerly employed as a chauffeur.

Ralph F. Robinson, of the Hussars, now in India, has spent some eight years in the Army, about five having been served in India.

Augustus M. B. Robinson, the next, is also in India, with the Wilts, and was for some time before the war in the employ of the Avon Indiarubber Company at Melksham.

Herbert J. Robinson, of the Household Cavalry, is at present in England. He was previously engaged in the butchering business, and also with the Avon Company.

The youngest, Edwin Robinson, is serving with the R.A.M.C. in France. Before joining up he was employed in the grocery trade at Calne.

Respecting the Avon Indiarubber Works, where the father is employed, as were three of the sons, it may not be out of place to add that, while a vast amount of Government work is turned out there, the number of male employées has been depleted by the removal of hundreds of men who have left the establishment to serve with the Colours.

[N.B.—By an error on the part of the engravers, the order of Irad and William is reversed, William, on the portrait, being No. 2 and Irad No. 3.]

Army Cyclist Corps

SPARKS Bertie

Australian Imperial Force

BREWER Harry
BREWER Herbert James
CROOK George
TYLER Charles Havelock

Bedfordshire Regiment

FARMER William George

Canadian Infantry

GAISFORD Frederick
VINCENT Raymond George

Canadian Mounted Rifles

BIGWOOD Wilfred Ewart

Coldstream Guards

CHANDLER Frederick George
EADES Ivan Stanley

Devonshire Regiment

BAGWELL Charles
CLARK Walter Samuel
DODIMEAD Albert Edward
FLOWER Sydney
GUNSTONE Frederick
HELLINGS Sidney Hugh
SKUSE Fred

Dragoon Guards (Queen's Bays)

WHITE George

Essex Regiment

DEVONISH Frederick Albert

Gloucestershire Regiment

MERCHANT Herbert John

Grenadier Guards

AMSBURY Daniel Pearce James
YOUNG William Henry

Hampshire Regiment

ASH Reginald
CROOK Cecil
WEBB Harry

Kings Royal Rifle Corps

DEVERALL Frederick Blake
OGLE Harry Charles

Kings Shropshire Light Infantry

ARTHURS Frank Stanley

Lancashire Fusiliers

HAYWARD Edwin George
TAYLOR Edward Forster
WEBB Charlie

Leinster Regiment

SCARLETT Walter

London
Post Office Rifles

BURBIDGE Walter Francis Victor

London
Rifle Brigade

DANCEY Luther William
DAY Ernest Alfred

London
Queen Victoria's Rifles

PHILLIPS Sidney George

London
London Scottish

CAMPBELL Harold Fletcher

London
Prince of Wales Own
Civil Service Rifles

GOULD Reginald Henry

Machine Gun Corps

GREGORY Ernest Albert
GREGORY John
HITCHENS Albert Edward

KEEN Roland John
MOBEY Francis Richard
SMITH Harry
TAYLOR Herbert
YOUNG Frederick

Mercantile Marine

ESCOTT William Lot

Middlesex Regiment

KAYNES Reginald Genvy

Norfolk Regiment

WHITE Alfred Ernest

North Staffordshire Regiment

ELLERY Robert James

Northumberland Fusiliers

WALLIS Kenneth Leslie Bilbrough

Royal Army Service Corps

BROWN Arthur Roland
BURBIDGE Thomas Harold
FRANKCOM Ronald Claude
HATHERALL William
OWEN J.A.

Rhodesia Regiment

SEWARD Harry

Royal Air Force

CLEVERLY William John

Royal Berkshire Regiment

BUCKLAND John Henry
MISSEN Frederick

Royal Engineers

HAWKINS Herbert John
NORRIS F.G.
ROGERS E.
SHARPE Harry
SPENCER William Frederick

Royal Field Artillery

ALLEN Percy Albert Gregory
ASH A.
BULL George
COTTLE Frederick James
LITTLE C.V.
MILNER Alfred Harry
PARFITT Herbert
RICKETTS Charles Stanley
SNOOK Reginald Charles

Royal Garrison Artillery

ASHBEE Frederick
SALTER Walter
SMITH Sydney Bicheno

Royal Irish Fusiliers

MATTOCK William Alfred

Royal Marine Artillery

DICKS William James
FERGUSON James Shaw

Royal Marine Light Infantry

CLIFFORD Arthur E
COLLETT Frank Stephen
ESCOTT Albert
PEARCE Robert Henry

Royal Navy

ALEXANDER Alfred Henry
BODMAN Herbert
FRY William Victor
FULLER Charles Edward
GORE Francis Cephus
GOSS Alfred John
GRANT Hedley Alexander
SHADWELL Frederick William
SHADWELL William Charles
TRIMMING Andrew

Royal Naval Division
Nelson Battalion

ALFORD John Henry

Royal Sussex Regiment

ELLIS Reginald Bertram

Royal Warwickshire Regiment

COOK William John
GREGORY Frank
WHITNEY Thomas Geffrey

Royal West Surrey Regiment

BARTON Frank Ernest

Royal Wiltshire Yeomanry

AWDRY Charles Selwyn D.S.O
SYDEE Frederick Percy

Somerset Light Infantry

ANNAL John Gerald
CANDY F.R.
HANCOCK Edward George
LINTHORN Bertram Charles
PROSSOR Frank Cecil
TRUEMAN William

South Wales Borderers

BODMAN John Cecil
PARSONS Arthur Leslie

Territorial Force Nursing Service

MARLEY Grace Margaret

Unknown Unit

Henry Hill

Welsh Regiment

RICKETTS Albert Charles

Wiltshire Regiment

ALFORD Victor Wallace
ATLAY John Keith
BAILEY Clifford Nelson
BAKER Victor
BARNES Charles
BARTHOLOMEW Henry George
BEAVEN Henry Sidney
BETHELL Henry James
BIGWOOD William Henry
BRITTAIN Albert Edward
BURBIDGE Andrew
CAINEY George
CARD D.H.
CHIVERS William Joseph

CLARK Ernest
COLLIER Albert Edward
COTTLE Bernard Newman
CURNICK George Christopher
DIFFELL William Frederick
EDWARDS William George
FRY Albert
GAY Walter Charles Frank
GAY William
GODWIN Arthur William
GOLDSBOROUGH Reginald Charles
GREGORY Edgar Jesse
GREGORY James
GUNSTONE William Henry
HAINES William Henry
HALE Ernest George
HARDING George Frederick
HARDY Adolphus Arthur Cyril
HARROLD Charles William Hayward
HAWKINS Alfred
HAWKINS Cornelius
HILLIER George
HILLIER Henry
HISCOX Arthur George
HORNBLOW Francis William
JONES Clifford Llewellyn
JONES Henry Thomas
KNEE Stanley George
LOCHHEAD Andrew
LODER William Victor
LOVE Samuel
MACE William George
MAGOR Arthur Curgenven
MALE Roy Douglas
MALE Walter
MANNING Geoffrey Hayward
MASLEN Ernest William
MERRETT W.F.
MISSEN Ernest William MM
NEWMAN Ralph
NICHOLSON William
OSBORN William Frank
PARK C.
PARK Sydney Alfred
PAYNE Francis Edgar
PEPLER A.S.
ROGERS Arthur
REYNOLDS Herbert Nelson
RICHARDS Frederick
SAWYER Frederick John
SHEPPARD Albert
SHEPPARD George
SMITH Alfred John
SPENCER William Herbert
TRIMNELL Albert
WAREHAM A.
WHITING Percy Louis

WILLIAMS Charles Frederick
WOOTTEN Albert Charles
WORSDELL D.F.
WYLDE George Richard

Worcestershire Regiment

MERRETT Arthur Stanley

RANDALL Percy Reginald
WALKER William Henry

York and Lancaster Regiment

SARTAIN Harry

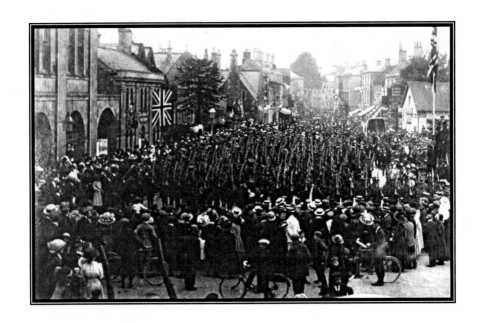

Armistice celebrations in Melksham Market Place
(Pictures courtesy Melksham and District Historical Society)